June 1,

Congratula ☑ W9-DEU-140

Aunt Sarah ☙

Uncle Scott

Jon Walker packs each daily devotion in *Growing with Purpose* with fresh insight and invigorating challenge. Wherever you are now with God, *Growing with Purpose* will provide you with a daily path to keep taking one step closer.

—Nancy Guthrie, author of
Hearing Jesus Speak into Your Sorrow

Eureka! I always knew he'd do it! Thirty-four years after I encouraged Jon Walker to become a writer, he's produced *Growing with Purpose*. I'm proud of his book and recommend it to you as thoughtful advice for the Christian soul.

—Dr. Judy Black, Jon's high school English teacher

In his new book, *Growing with Purpose*, Jon Walker eloquently serves up bite-sized nuggets of God's truth wrapped in a relevant simplicity that encourages and replenishes the reader. *Growing with Purpose* is a breath of fresh air in the world of devotionals.

—Mary Southerland, author/speaker

Growing with Purpose: It's like a close friend whispering from day to day, "Let me talk to you for a moment." The friend speaks truth, and he speaks it with a loving heart. Each day as I venture out, I am thankful for my friend's nurture of my soul.

—Art Toalston, editor of Baptist Press

Jon writes with a tender heart and a strong conviction that will strengthen you to live the daily life of faith.

— Tom Holladay, teaching pastor at Saddleback Church, and author, *The Relationship Principles of Jesus*

If knowing who God is and where God is determines how we live our lives, then *Growing with Purpose* by Jon Walker will invite its readers to live differently … purposefully … with a growing passion to know God and be a purer expression of his life.

— Steve Pettit, director, One In Christ, Inc.

Jon Walker provides 365 different angles from which to view God. By doing so, he moves us a little closer to understanding two things we never fully grasp — God's greatness and his grace toward undeserving sinners. I highly recommend it this book.

— Dr. Alan Godwin, psychologist, author of *How to Solve Your People Problems: Dealing with Your Difficult Relationships*

Jon Walker's book causes me to think; it makes me yearn for spiritual depth. I rarely find both qualities in a devotional book.

— Cecil Murphey, author or coauthor of more than 100 books, including the *New York Times* bestsellers *90 Minutes in Heaven* and *Heaven Is Rea.*

Growing with PURPOSE

Connecting with God Every Day

Jon Walker

ZONDERVAN.com/
AUTHOR**TRACKER**
follow your favorite authors

ZONDERVAN

Growing with Purpose
Copyright © 2009 by Jon Walker

This title is also available as a Zondervan ebook.
Visit www.zondervan.com/ebooks.

This title is also available in a Zondervan audio edition.
Visit www.zondervan.fm.

Requests for information should be addressed to:

Zondervan, *Grand Rapids, Michigan 49530*

Library of Congress Cataloging-in-Publication Data

Walker, Jon, 1958-
      Growing with purpose: connecting with God every day / Jon Walker.
         p.   cm.
      Includes bibliographical references and indexes.
      ISBN 978-0-310-29213-5 (hardcover)
      1. Devotional calendars. I. Title.
BV4811.W325 2009
    242'.2—dc22   2009018574

Published in association with Rosenbaum & Associates Literary Agency, Brentwood, Tennessee.

Interior design by Michelle Espinoza

Printed in the United States of America

---

09 10 11 12 13 14 • 20 19 18 17 16 15 14 13 12 11 10 9 8 7 6 5 4 3 2 1

For Christopher and Nathan
My inheritance becomes yours.

CONTENTS

ACKNOWLEDGMENTS

It's impossible to write any book without acknowledging, like Tennyson, "I am part of all that I have met." That being the case, it would be impossible to thank everyone, but I do want to mention these few: Steve Pettit and Rick Warren have both mentored me in their own ways, and their influence permeates this text. My thanks also to Lori Hensley, Ed Walker, Sherry Walker, Kathy Chapman Sharp, Carolyn Baker, Doug Hart, Mark Kelly, Oswald Chambers, Ian Thomas, Rich Mullins, Paul Carlisle, Mark Tabb, Judy Black, Sally Killian, Anita Zelek, Kathy Melilli, Elizabeth John, Sue Brower, Verlyn D. Verbrugge, Debbie Head, Bucky Rosenbaum, and Susan Goetz.

FOREWORD
Rick Warren

For almost ten years, Jon Walker worked behind the scenes at Saddleback Church and Purpose Driven Ministries. He helped me launch Pastors.com, one of the first Christian websites on the Internet, and became the founding editor of my online newsletter, *Rick Warren's Ministry ToolBox*.

As I came to know Jon, I realized his gift for writing combined the insight of a novelist with the practicality of a teacher, and that his desire to communicate clearly emerged from a call to explain how God's grace transforms our lives. When Jon told me he sensed God's call to a new phase of his life, I wasn't surprised; I'd seen the restlessness in him.

But I was really pleased to hear that he wanted to continue work with the Purpose Driven Life daily devotionals. You will find Jon's devotionals make the message of God's grace clear and practical.

Jon would be the first to tell you that he learned these truths from others and that he is simply being faithful to pass them on to you. We both hope that you will apply these truths in your life and pass them on to others, just as the apostle Paul taught Timothy: "Now teach these truths to other trustworthy people who will be able to pass them on to others" (2 Timothy 2:2b NLT).

God created you for his purposes and this book of devotionals will encourage you to live a purpose driven life day in and day out. I am praying for you and know you will be successful as you commit to God's plan.

HOLINESS IS A
REASONABLE REQUEST

"Be holy, because I am holy."
1 Peter 1:16

There are days when I think I'm doing pretty well in my pursuit of holiness; other days, I find myself in the dirt, the mud and crud of life all over my fallen-world face.

On those less-than-saintly days, I wonder if Peter was engaged in wishful thinking when he restated God's call from Leviticus that we are to be holy, just as our heavenly Father is holy (1 Peter 1:16).

Yet, Ian Thomas says our call to holiness is a perfectly reasonable request. Isaiah's vision of heaven reveals what this means: He looks around and says, in effect, "All that I've done hasn't come anywhere near to covering my guilt and sin. Lord, I cannot match your holiness" (see Isaiah 6:5; 64:6).

Just then, one of the seraphs flies to Isaiah with a glowing hot coal from heaven's altar, and says, "See, this has touched your lips; your guilt is taken away and your sin atoned for" (Isaiah 6:7).

The thing to remember today, and forever, is that God initiates your cleansing and it is God, not your efforts, who makes you holy.

I Can't, God Can

Not that we are competent in ourselves to claim anything
for ourselves, but our competence comes from God.
2 Corinthians 3:5

My buddy Paul Carlisle says you have to confess "I can't" before you can agree that God can. The danger is, if we rush past "I can't," we will never fully embrace the notion that only God can.

We will just keep thinking there's still some ability (sufficiency) in us. We will continue to believe, wrongly, that we can do some things, perhaps all things, apart from God. We will lock into a mythology that if we keep all the rules, or even just a few of the rules, we've somehow made ourselves into good little Christians.

Being Spirit-led means you recognize that the rules written on stone are external and separate from who we are. Therefore, they are inferior to God's complete intention; his plan is to write the new rules onto your heart with his very own hand.

God does this through the work of the Holy Spirit, who is working inside you, transforming you into a reflection of Jesus Christ.

Was Jesus a man led by rules or led by God's Spirit? And how would you answer that question for you?

THE GOD-CHIP

I pray that out of his glorious riches he may strengthen you with power through his Spirit in your inner being, so that Christ may dwell in your hearts through faith.
Ephesians 3:16–17

God empowers you to successfully do everything he asks you to do. He transforms you inwardly with a growing desire to serve others and then he gives you abilities to use in sacri-service to others.

The Holy Spirit within gives you the ability to tune into God—to hear him, to listen to him, and to talk with him. So, please hear this: God didn't create you to fail; he created you to succeed once the Holy Spirit energizes your abilities and empowers your efforts.

Perhaps you've noticed the small stickers on many computers that say, "Powered by [this brand of chip]." In a sense, you have the "God-chip" powering your life as a follower of Christ. You are empowered by the one and only holy God, who has placed his Holy Spirit within you.

God energizes you to live like Jesus. In faith, believe God enables you to succeed. Tell God your fears and ask him to replace your fears with faith.

It's the "Wow!" Not the How

*Suddenly a great company of the heavenly host appeared
with the angel, praising God and saying, "Glory to God in the
highest, and on earth peace to men on whom his favor rests."*
Luke 2:13–14

My friend and spiritual mentor, Steve Pettit, says that in
our well-intentioned focus on the "how" of Christianity, we
often lose sight of the "wow!"—that God's Holy Spirit lives
within us until the very end of time.

Say this with me, brothers and sisters:

- Wow! The God who spoke the world into existence
  also spoke me into existence! (Genesis 1)
- Wow! The God of creation shaped me as a masterpiece,
  crafted for the mission of proclaiming his "wow!" (Jeremiah 1:5)
- Wow! The God who placed the moon, stars, and the
  sun in the sky also placed his Holy Spirit within me!
  (Romans 8:11)
- Wow! The God who owns the cattle on a thousand
  hills considers me one of his heirs and is pleased to give
  me a share in his kingdom! (Psalm 51:10; Luke 12:32)

It's not the "how"; it's the "wow!"

HELP MY UNBELIEF!

"I do believe; help me overcome my unbelief!"
Mark 9:24

Recently, I've been thinking this should be my life verse.

I do believe, yet I have so much unbelief in my life. I walk in faith, yet my faith is often more in the things I see than in the things I don't see. I follow God, yet I repeatedly find myself stumbling down a path of my own choosing.

Oswald Chambers says, "Living a life of faith means never knowing where you are being led. But it does mean loving and knowing the One who is leading. It is literally a life of faith, not of understanding and reason—a life of knowing him who calls us to go." I believe. God, help me overcome my unbelief:

- I believe. Help me live like I believe.
- I believe. Help me choose like I believe.
- I believe. Help me trust like I believe.

Help me to live like I deeply believe you are trustworthy. Help me to abandon my mythology where I believe I am more trustworthy than you, where I live with more faith in my own efforts than in your ability to create the universe.

GOD MEANT IT FOR GOOD

*"You intended to harm me, but God intended it for good
to accomplish what is now being done."*
Genesis 50:20

Joseph's life was anything but peaceful. He was sold into slavery by jealous brothers and thrown into prison on false charges. Yet, he remained free of bitterness or regret and saw God as the Great Engineer behind even the worst of circumstances.

The theology packed in Joseph's statement above is astounding. "God intended it for good" says:

You can accept the past. No sin, no action, no choice on your part is too big for God to handle or too big to be worked for the good of those who love him (Romans 8:28).

You can embrace the present. There is no need to play the "what if" game. The past is forgiven and gone and the future is in God's omnipotent hands. You are free to focus on loving God with all your heart, soul, and mind (Romans 8:38).

You can look expectantly toward the future. Even if you make mistakes today, God still controls your future. Even when things appear to be terrible, you can trust that God is working out his divine plan through you—and his plan is good (Jeremiah 29:11).

MAKING THE CHOICE TO SIN

*For sin shall not be your master, because you
are not under law, but under grace.*
Romans 6:14

When comedian Dana Carvey imitated George H. W. Bush, he would say, "Not gonna do it, not gonna do it!"

We can say the same to sin. When we face temptation, we have the power of the Holy Spirit within us to make the right decision—but the choice is still ours.

The problem is most of us live thinking we have no choice but to sin.

You can see this in people with addictions. They believe the lie that they have no choice but to feed their addictions, and then this erroneous belief guides their behavior.

But Paul says sin is no longer natural to us. It was natural for the old you, but it is *not* natural for the new you, who is alive in Christ.

The blood of Jesus Christ broke the power of sin in our lives. We do have the ability—being empowered by God's Holy Spirit—to say, "Not gonna do it anymore."

LOOK UPON THE THINGS ABOVE

Set your minds on things above, not on earthly things.
Colossians 3:2

Let's assume there is a long, thin line threaded across reality. My friend Steve Pettit suggests this imaginary line divides what we can see from what we cannot see — the temporary from the eternal.

Paul says we should set our minds on those things above this line and not on the earthly things below it.

With our minds set on the things above, we live in the truth that there is more to reality than the things right in front of us. We live in the truth that people are eternal beings and decisions that seemed insignificant, when seen in the fullness of reality, are of eternal significance.

Eugene Peterson paraphrases Colossians 3:2 this way in *The Message*: "Don't shuffle along, eyes to the ground, absorbed with the things right in front of you. Look up, and be alert to what is going on around Christ — that's where the action is. See things from his perspective."

Our objective-in-Jesus is to look upon the things above so that we can understand that what we see and feel is not a full and accurate measurement of God's reality. Seeing things this way will change how we live.

A WASTEFUL AND EXTRAVAGANT LOVE

"The older brother became angry and refused to go in.
So his father went out and pleaded with him."
Luke 15:28

If you look up the word *prodigal* in the dictionary, you are likely to see a picture of the prodigal son sitting in the mud sharing a meal with pigs. He dines with swine because he has blown through his entire inheritance—being a prodigal means you are wastefully extravagant.

Yet, the older brother in this story argues that his father is the one who is truly extravagant because he throws away blessings on the youngest son.

The oldest looks with judgment on his father, demanding he limit his compassion toward the younger son. Yet, the truth is, the father was just as joyfully extravagant with his oldest son: "My son," the father told him, "you are always with me, and everything I have is yours" (Luke 15:31).

When we insist God limit his extravagant compassion with others, we limit the abundant, extravagant compassion he gives to us: "For in the same way you judge others, you will be judged, and with the measure you use, it will be measured to you" (Matthew 7:2).

RADIANT CERTAINTY

*"Now is your time of grief, but I will see you again and
you will rejoice, and no one will take away your joy."*
John 16:22

There are some days when, frankly, I don't feel much like
worshiping God. There are probably more days like that than
I'd care to admit.

Usually those are days when I'm staring at my circumstances and I struggle with the God-truth that he is in the
circumstances surrounding my life — *all* the circumstances.

Jesus was so sure that God's faithfulness would be present
in all circumstances that his certainty radiated throughout his
whole being. Heading into a crisis that would ultimately cost
him his life, at the Last Supper Jesus exhibited such radiant
certainty about God's faithfulness that not one of his disciples
discerned his death was lurking outside the door.

We, also, can have this radiant certainty about God's
hand in our lives. We can say, "When it comes to God's faithfulness, I know because I know that I know."

JESUS CLEANSES AND CALLS

"I am ruined! For I am a man of unclean lips."
Isaiah 6:5

One of the most effective tools the enemy will use to keep you from serving God is convincing you that you've either messed up too much or that you must clean up your life before you can get God's attention. When these thoughts pop into your head, sniff the air for the scent of sulfur because these are lies straight from the fires of hell!

If you follow the sequence of Isaiah 6, you'll see how God initiates the process that brings you into his holy presence and purifies you to remain in his presence. You will also see that your new guilt-free, sin-atoned status will compel you and prepare you for the unique mission God sets before you.

God's intention when he convicts us of our sins is not to condemn us. Rather, his breath of life disperses the "fog of war"—that satanic smoke the father of lies uses to keep us on the run from God.

But God wants us to run to him with our sin. His holy fire will burn the mess away and then seal within you the work of Jesus Christ.

VISION CHANGES
THE WAY YOU LIVE

For the vision is yet for an appointed time.
Habakkuk 2:3 (NKJV)

Perhaps the most powerful aspect of vision is that it changes your way of thinking; that, in turn, changes the way you live.

I met two brothers living off a vision. Neither of them had a steady job. Both still lived with their parents and they relied on handouts from others to keep it all together.

These brothers didn't have real jobs because they were constantly touring as a Christian band. They lived with mom and dad because their parents knew it would save them money and the "handouts" were donations from others who believed in their music ministry.

The power of God's vision sustained them as they got older and all their friends began to settle down. Eventually, the music of Brad and Todd Olsen was nominated for a Christian music Dove award. Their band, The Waiting, patiently *waited* for the vision's "appointed time."

The vision God places in front of you is "yet for an appointed time," but you can live with a radiant certainty that its time will come.

THE SAME SPIRIT AT WORK

*For through him we both have access
to the Father by one Spirit.*
Ephesians 2:18

In a time long ago and a land far, far away, I found myself frustrated one day with a coworker. My sweet southern aunt might say this coworker was being *contrary*.

Did I mention that my coworker and I were in ministry together working for the global glory of God? Soon, I realized the real source of my frustration was simply our inability to get along, even though the same Spirit at work in me is the same Spirit at work in him (James 4:5).

Catch that? *The same Spirit at work in me is the same Spirit at work in him.*

The same Spirit at work in you is the same Spirit at work in me. We are temples of the Holy Spirit, but the dirty windows in our temple suppress the Spirit's light shining within us (1 Corinthians 6:19).

But take heart, you who colabor with me. Be encouraged that the Spirit God placed within us both is constantly at work, washing our windows and sweeping out the cobwebs, changing us for God's glory and his pleasure.

BEHAVIOR EXPOSING BELIEF

Did you receive the Spirit by observing the law,
or by believing what you heard?
Galatians 3:2–3

The apostle Paul, who struggled with legalism, taught the Galatians that the law was only put in charge to "lead us to Christ that we might be justified by faith. Now that faith has come, we are no longer under the supervision of the law" (Galatians 3:24–25).

The law is not in charge of our lives; it is meant to show us the futility of trying to earn our way into God's good graces. We are transformed, not by the law, but by the Spirit of the living God, who in his own hand writes his will upon our hearts where it cannot be lost, diminished, forgotten, or ignored (2 Corinthians 3:3).

Like the Galatians, we are often fools. After being cleansed by the blood of the Lamb and embedded with the Holy Spirit, we return to the errant belief that godly goals are reached by extra-human effort (Galatians 3:1–5).

Simply saying we believe something does not mean that we really believe it. The way we behave reveals what we believe deep in our hearts.

ANGER MANAGEMENT

For man's anger does not bring about
the righteous life that God desires.
James 1:20

Your anger will not bring about any long-term change in your wife, your husband, your friend, or your next-door neighbor (or even that obnoxious coworker).

Believe it or not, the Holy Spirit is perfectly capable of leaning on others, convincing them to change their ways, to do the right thing. It takes faith to believe this.

If you're like me, though, you keep assuming God needs your help; that a little anger on your part will bring about the "righteous life that God desires" (James 1:20).

Most of the time my anger emerges from mixed motives (James 4:1 – 3). It is self-righteous anger, or perhaps a better description is unrighteous anger. But my unrighteous behavior will not bring about godly, righteous living.

The truth is our anger will not get others to act, think, believe, or live like we want them to — or to act like Jesus. Our anger may change their behavior in the short run, but it doesn't change what is in their hearts.

Our objective-in-Jesus is to love others and leave it up to the Holy Spirit to change them.

LOVE THAT SWEATS

We continually remember before our God and Father
your work produced by faith, your labor prompted by love,
and your endurance inspired by hope in our Lord Jesus Christ.
1 Thessalonians 1:3

When Jesus loves, he works up a sweat; he rolls up his sleeves, gets on his knees, and washes our feet with his blood, sweat, and tears.

He labors at love, though his love is never like labor. He is a giver and loves us until we can take no more because we are filled to overflowing—his love spilling through us into the cores of those we love with his love, a love labor not lost on a world that needs to be found.

Jesus wrestles our fears, wrangles with our doubts, and labors at love until he is exhausted. He even lay prone in a garden and drank the necessary nourishment from God's cup for one last heroic but sweaty, bloody, and tearful lift of the Father's infinite love. He was ready to die to give us God's undying love.

Your objective-in-Jesus is to grow confident that Jesus, compelled by a love that lasts forever, is laboring in and through you to finish what he started in you (John 13:1).

BLIND TRUTH: EYES WIDE OPEN

"This happened so that the work of God
might be displayed in his life."
John 9:3

As Jesus and his school-in-motion moved through town, they came upon a man who had been blind since birth. The disciples started to blame someone: "Maybe he's blind because he sinned? Maybe he's blind because of something his parents did?"

Jesus' response has been paraphrased, "You're asking the wrong question. You're looking for someone to blame. There is no such cause-effect here. Look instead for what God can do" (John 9:3–4 MSG).

Look instead for what God can do!

Get your eyes off the things below and look to what God can do right now through you, because the "night is coming" when you'll no longer be able to work (John 9:4).

We don't have time to assign blame or to figure it all out. Instead we need to ask, "What do you want me to do in this situation, Lord? I'm still a student in Christ's school-in-motion—what are you teaching me?"

A Not-to-Do List

So let's keep focused on that goal, those of us who want
everything God has for us. If any of you have something else
in mind, something less than total commitment, God will
clear your blurred vision—you'll see it yet! Now that
we're on the right track, let's stay on it.
Philippians 3:15 – 16 (MSG)

Imagine if God created you to be the Michelangelo of
this age, but you stayed so busy doing all kinds of things—
good things—that you never got around to painting and
sculpting.

You would end up missing the best because you got dis-
tracted chasing the good.

What a disappointment it would be for God, you, and
all the people who would have been blessed if you had stayed
focused on your original purpose!

Today, instead of making a to-do list, make a not-to-
do list. Fill your not-to-do list with things you do that don't
match God's purpose for your life, and press on toward the
goal to win the prize for which God has called you (Philippians 3:14).

No Longer Shaped by Fear

"If you love those who love you, what credit is that to you?
Even 'sinners' love those who love them."
Luke 6:32

Our objective-in-Jesus is to love the unlovable and this makes the Christian community unique. God insists that love should set the agenda for our lives; yet, we so often insist that fear set the agenda.

In fear, we look out for ourselves and behave similar to those who are unloving and those who are ungodly. Fear terrorizes us so we remain emotionally immature and spiritually isolated. Fear holds us hostage, keeping us from developing authentic, transparent relationships.

God created us so that if we live a self-absorbed life we will fail every time, using our methods of self-service, self-preservation, and self-determination.

Instead, God says, in essence, "Love one another in the same way that I have loved you." Impossible?

God is already at work in us, dismantling the barricades we have built for self-protection. His objective is to love the fear out of us so it will no longer shape our lives, and so we can then love the fear out of others.

YOUR OWN GENESIS WEEK

Now the earth was formless and empty, darkness was over
the surface of the deep, and the Spirit of God was
hovering over the waters. And God said . . .
Genesis 1:2–3

God spoke the world into existence, and he spoke you into your mother's womb. Even now, he can speak into the "chaos of [your] life" to bring it shape and form (Psalm 51:10 MSG).

This is a Genesis event, when God speaks into the void and the darkness of your life, creating a new beginning for you.

God wants to see you pure, so he takes an active role in creating your new heart. He can create something from nothing; he can take a heart that is broken or misdirected and create a heart that is whole and purposeful.

Your job is to submit to his sovereignty, humble yourself before him, and ask for his help.

Lord, speak a Genesis moment into our hearts and into the circumstances of our lives. We acknowledge "everything that we have—right thinking and right living, a clean slate and a fresh start—comes from God by way of Jesus Christ" (1 Corinthians 1:30 MSG).

LOVE IS A CHOICE WE MAKE

*"A new command I give you: Love one another.
As I have loved you, so you must love one another."*
John 13:34

Our objective-in-Jesus is to *choose* to love one another. We are to actively, consistently, and deeply love other believers regardless of how we feel about them, how unlovable they may appear, or how difficult it may seem.

The apostle John views love and obedience as synonymous: If you love Jesus, you will obey his commands (John 14:15, 23–24; 15:12, 14, 17; 1 John 2:5; 5:3; 2 John 1:6).

Why is obedience connected with love? Because it reflects that we have lined up our thoughts and plans with God's to make them one with his, and it brings us into a submission where we only do and say what the Father tells us to do and say.

Christ pushes the definition of love to a higher level, a level that combines behavior and beliefs into godly action. Love is shown when a mother stumbles to her baby's crib for the fifth time in one night, or a passenger gives up his place on a lifeboat to save someone else from a sinking ship. Love is Christ on a cross, dying for us.

Love is a choice we make (Romans 5:8).

ENGINEER AT WORK

While Peter was wondering about the meaning of the vision,
the men sent by Cornelius ... stopped at the gate.
Acts 10:17

Peter is praying when he sees a vision of forbidden food. He recoils, saying, "I have never eaten anything impure or unclean" (Acts 10:14). A heavenly voice says, "Do not call anything impure that God has made clean" (Acts 10:15).

In another town God had told Cornelius, a centurion, a Gentile, and in a figurative sense forbidden food, to look for a man named Peter. So Cornelius had sent three men to find him.

As the men approach the house where Peter is praying, the Holy Spirit tells Peter, "Simon, three men are looking for you" (Acts 10:19). Peter follows the men to Cornelius's house and finds a crowd waiting to hear the good news.

Cornelius tells Peter that God promised to send him a messenger. Instantly, Peter understands that he is that messenger and that his vision was a perfectly timed lesson from the Almighty that the gospel is for all people, even Gentiles.

Oswald Chambers describes God as the Great Engineer, creating circumstances to bring about divine appointments in our lives. Watch today for how God engineers divine encounters in your life.

The Waiting Is
the Hardest Part

Now Sarai, Abram's wife, had borne him no children ...
so she said to Abram, "The LORD has kept me
from having children. Go, sleep with my maidservant;
perhaps I can build a family through her."
Genesis 16:1–2

Sarai waited and waited for God to provide their first descendant, to answer her prayers, to make good on his promise — but the baby didn't come.

Perhaps, like you or like me, Sarai began to wonder if God would ever answer her prayers or if he had forgotten about her, whether he really knew what he was doing.

Sarai acknowledged God's ability to fulfill his promise of providing her with a child; yet, like many of us, she questioned God's sovereignty to decide when and how that promise would be fulfilled.

If we could ask Sarai, "Can God?" she most likely would answer "Yes." If we then asked Sarai, "Will God?" her honest answer may have been "No."

When faced with a delayed answer, what do your actions say about your belief in God?

WALKING WITH A BROKEN LEG

Now that faith has come,
we are no longer under the supervision of the law.
Galatians 3:25

Suppose that one day you see me wearing a huge cast on my leg and I explain I have a pretty serious injury. I have to wear the cast for at least three months.

But then, about a year later you see me still wearing the same cast and you say, "I thought that cast was supposed to retrain you to walk after your accident."

I reply, "Oh, the cast. The doctor wanted to take it off after three months, but I wouldn't let him. It's gotten pretty comfortable to walk on, and between you and me, it's frightening to think about walking without the cast."

Consider this: The cast is the law, and the law is meant to teach us how to walk with God after Jesus performs surgery on us to heal our sin-wounds.

There is nothing evil about the cast. God created it to help us walk again. But it was never meant to be a permanent solution. The Spirit inside us is the long-term solution to walking the way God wants us to walk.

JESUS PRAYS FOR YOU

"My prayer is not for them alone. I pray also for those who will believe in me through their message."
John 17:20

During the Last Supper, Jesus prayed for himself and then he prayed for the disciples. And then, with the hour of his death approaching, he took time to pray for you:

"Father, just as you are in me and I am in you. May they also be in us so that the world may believe that you have sent me. I have given them the glory that you gave me, that they may be one as we are one: I in them and you in me. May they be brought to complete unity to let the world know that you sent me and have loved them even as you have loved me.

"Father, I want those you have given me to be with me where I am, and to see my glory, the glory you have given me because you loved me before the creation of the world." (John 17:21–24)

Think upon this: You were in his mind when Jesus prayed this prayer.

THE HOLY SPIRIT NUDGE

The man without the Spirit does not accept the things
that come from the Spirit of God ... he cannot understand
them, because they are spiritually discerned.
1 Corinthians 2:14

When I located a book I'd been searching for on the library shelf, I was jazzed. But as I approached the front desk, I felt the Holy Spirit check me.

I looked at the book's cover and it didn't give a clue as to why the Spirit was prompting me not to read it. I thought about ignoring the Spirit's direction.

Like a child, I weighed the pros and cons of disobedience, and then put the book back on the shelf. My hesitant obedience emerged from my memory of standing too many times on the wrong side of God's direction.

Isn't that what faith is? Trusting God when he tells us that reading what appears to be a harmless book will take us somewhere he doesn't want us to go.

The Spirit is teaching us to think and act like Jesus. He nudges, prompts, rebukes, and protects us as God writes the law into our hearts.

OBJECTIVE-IN-JESUS: LOOK FOR THE BEST

Look for the best in each other,
and always do your best to bring it out.
1 Thessalonians 5:15 (MSG)

Bringing out the best in others begins with our willingness to look for the good in them. If we stay focused on their negative traits or their weaknesses, we eventually blind ourselves to their God-crafted potential. When we constantly point to their faults while failing to applaud their virtues, we bring out the worst in them. We do the same when we expect people to fail or when we swing to the other side, expecting them to be perfect.

When we approach others in a way that "always protects, always trusts, always hopes, always perseveres" (1 Corinthians 13:7), we not only encourage the best in them, we also tell them that we are there to give and not to take. Our objective-in-Jesus is to catch others in the act of doing good, and then to encourage them to keep doing good.

You can choose to bring out the best in others. Start today by salting your conversations with phrases such as: "I believe in you"; "I'm grateful for you"; "I see God using you"; "I appreciate you"; and "I'm glad you're in my life."

YOKED COMPANIONS
OF COMPASSION

Are you tired? Worn out? Burned out on religion?
Come to me. Get away with me and you'll recover your life.
I'll show you how to take a real rest ... I won't
lay anything heavy or ill-fitting on you.
Matthew 11:28–30 (MSG)

Most translations of Matthew 11:28–30 refer to the easy "yoke" of Jesus—"Take my yoke upon you." But Eugene Peterson's paraphrase above captures the spirit of Jesus' teaching.

Jesus is looking for companions of compassion. He wants us to journey with him and get to know him, not run off to do things for him while we ignore him.

"Aren't you tired and burned out on all that religious stuff, anyway?" Jesus, in a sense, asks. "Look, come walk with me, and I'll help you take back your *life*, your real purpose. And even though it'll require some hard, very hard work, you'll be energized by it because you'll be living a life of abundance. You'll be doing exactly what our Father created you to do, and more importantly, you'll be exactly who I want you to be."

FAITH EXPRESSED AS LOVE

*"Which of these three do you think was a neighbor
to the man who fell into the hands of robbers?" The expert
in the law replied, "The one who had mercy on him."
Jesus told him, "Go and do likewise."*
Luke 10:36–37

As I waited with family and friends for my father to come out of open heart surgery, the Holy Spirit nudged me toward a frail Hispanic man sitting alone in the far corner of the waiting room. His wife had diabetes and the surgeons were removing both her legs. He not only feared for her life; he wondered how they would get by now.

Because so many others were looking out for the needs of my father, I sensed God was telling me to help this man. So I spent time praying with him and connecting him with a local congregation, a social worker, and other forms of support.

In faith, I knew my father was in God's hands. I also knew my family was meeting my father's needs. This allowed me to be faithful as an instrument of God's love to another. Jesus told us, "Go and do likewise."

God designed this life to sever our ties to self-centeredness and to teach us to put the needs of others before our own. Our objective-in-Jesus is to live in this truth: "The only thing that counts is faith expressing itself through love" (Galatians 5:6).

INTERCEDE OR CRITICIZE?

And pray in the Spirit on all occasions with all kinds of prayers and requests. With this in mind, be alert and always keep on praying for all the saints.
Ephesians 6:18

Oswald Chambers says in *My Utmost for His Highest*: "When we discern that other people are not growing spiritually and allow that discernment to turn to criticism, we block our fellowship with God. God never gives us discernment so that we may criticize, but that we may intercede."

We should take our concerns about another believer to God, praying on behalf of our brother or sister. This doesn't mean we ignore or deny the fault we see, but it does mean we look past it to identify the need that is *feeding* the fault.

The discernment God gives us is a prayer alert. *Woe unto us* if we use that discernment in a self-centered manner, such as pointing a finger.

The discernment God gives us is meant to push us toward other-centered prayer, where our objective-in-Jesus is to pray for them in the Spirit of "love, joy, peace, patience, kindness, goodness, faithfulness, gentleness and self-control" (Galatians 5:22 – 23).

how we should pray

CHRIST, THE CURRICULUM

But you have not so learned Christ.
Ephesians 4:20 (NKJV)

In the school of Christ, Jesus is the curriculum.

We are to learn Christ, being "taught in him in accordance with the truth that is in Jesus" (Ephesians 4:21). Since he is the Truth and all truth is in him, we must know him to teach others about him (Colossians 1:28). Otherwise, it's like trying to tell someone about fine Italian dining when your only experience is eating spaghetti out of cans.

So many of us live on canned spaghetti and yet we wonder why life with Jesus tastes so much like leftovers. We approach God's Word as if it merely dispenses facts, yet we wonder why our knowledge seems like hollow wisdom.

All the while, Jesus calls us to attend his school, saying, "You search the Scriptures because you believe they give you eternal life. But the Scriptures point to me! Yet you refuse to come to me to receive this life" (John 5:39–40 NLT).

NEVER LEAVING THE GARAGE

I can do everything through him who gives me strength.
Philippians 4:13

Faith is acting in confidence that God's power is active in and through your life; faith is trusting God's power will be your strength to do everything through him.

When you say, "There's something I'd really like to do for God, but I don't think that I can do it," God may reply, "Great! I'm glad you've figured it out. You can't do it by yourself, but with my power working through you, you can do anything I ask you to do."

If you only say, "I can't," and never recognize that "God can," you are less likely to even attempt great things for God. It's like having a car with the most powerful engine ever built, but saying, "I don't think it can get me past the first intersection." So you leave it in your garage, never taking it onto the road.

God's power is available to you: "For God is working in you, giving you the desire and the power to do what pleases him" (Philippians 2:13 NLT).

NO MORE BLEEDING
ON THE SABBATH

"There are six days for work. So come and be healed
on those days, not on the Sabbath."
Luke 13:14

Imagine you have just stopped by your neighbor's house for a quick visit and while you're chatting in the den, her toddler trips, hits his head on the sharp edge of a coffee table, and begins bleeding profusely. As you rush to help the child, you hear the boy's mother behind you screaming, "Oh no! He's ruined my carpet!"

If the story were true, you'd be pretty angry that the mother was more concerned about carpet than about her injured son.

The problem Jesus had with the Pharisees was that, in a sense, they were more concerned about carpets than children. They placed a higher value on rules and regulations than they did on the people they were supposed to shepherd and love.

When Jesus was chastised for rushing to the aid of bleeding children, the local leader of such lists of rules essentially said, "Those of you who are bleeding, come back tomorrow!"

Our objective-in-Jesus is to learn to love others twenty-four hours a day, seven days a week.

From Selfishness to Otherness

Nobody should seek his own good, but the good of others.
1 Corinthians 10:24

The other day my sister was feeling homesick and was perplexed because she was at home. She prayed, and as she did so the Spirit led her to pray for her son, who was on the mission field.

When she told me, my first thought was, "This is how our transformation in Jesus takes place." We become other-centered, even to the point that when the Holy Spirit nudges us to prayer, we search for whom we should pray for, rather than assuming we should only pray for our personal needs.

God did not place the Spirit within us simply to meet our own needs. He placed the Spirit within us to share him with others, ultimately leading them to ask God to place the Spirit in them, that is, receive Jesus into their hearts.

God fills us with himself to give us the ability to empty ourselves of self-interest and make the interests and concerns of others our greater priority.

GOD IS NEVER FAIR

The LORD is compassionate and gracious, slow to anger,
abounding in love ... he does not treat us as our sins deserve.
Psalm 103:8, 10

My boys are obsessed with fairness. They argue over who gets the biggest piece, who gets to play the computer game the longest, and who gets to sit next to the window. I suspect your children or other children you know are the same.

But we adults argue too: "Let me have the bigger slice"; "Let me have the better salary"; "Let me get away with it this time."

We argue with God in the same way, saying that we want fairness when we're really asking for special treatment. God could respond: "I'm a holy God and you've done some very unholy things. Fair means I can stay angry at you forever and punish you for the horrible things you've done. Do you really want fair?"

While we plead for fairness, God pursues us with an unfailing, unfair love: "He does not punish us for all our sins; he does not deal harshly with us, as we deserve" (Psalm 103:10 NLT).

God is never fair, and we are grateful this is true.

TRUTH: GOD IS STRONG AND HE WANTS ME STRONG

And that about wraps it up.
God is strong, and he wants you strong.
Ephesians 6:10 (MSG)

In faith, I know this to be true:

God is strong, and he wants me strong.

Though I am weak, God will make me strong because he is strong.

Though I am exhausted, God will make me strong because he is strong.

God is strong and he wants me strong to go where he wants me to go: "Be strong and very courageous ... do not turn from it to the right or to the left, that you may be successful wherever you go" (Joshua 1:7).

God is strong and his commandments give me "the strength to go in and take over the land" (Deuteronomy 11:8).

God is strong and he makes me strong, knowing that he is with me always: "Be strong and courageous. Do not be afraid or terrified because of them, for the LORD your God goes with you; he will never leave you nor forsake you" (Deuteronomy 31:6).

GOD'S LOVE ALWAYS SUCCEEDS

Follow the way of love.
1 Corinthians 14:1

In the garden of Gethsemane, when Jesus abandoned his own will and submitted to the Father's will, he placed his faith in the one whose love always wins.

Days later, the resurrection validated Jesus' faith in the Father's undefeatable love.

The truth is, God's love is unstoppable — it always succeeds and it always gets the final word. The apostle Paul described it from the other direction, saying, "Love never fails" (1 Corinthians 13:8).

When our love faithfully rests in the Father's undefeatable love, our capacity to know and to then express the win-win nature of God's love is enlarged. What this means is that, guided by the Holy Spirit, we intentionally "keep right on loving others as long as life lasts" (Hebrews 6:11 LB).

God's love is flowing through us and will never fail. We may not see the final outcome — our sight may even suggest our love was wasted — but we live by faith in the one whose love always succeeds.

JESUS LAUGHING

*Jesus said, "Let the little children come to me,
and do not hinder them, for the kingdom of heaven
belongs to such as these."*
Matthew 19:14

Back in the 1960s, *Playboy* magazine printed a drawing of Jesus—laughing. Although their corporate philosophy stood counter to God, their point was that Jesus must have been joyful because who would be attracted to a frowning, judgmental teacher?

In truth, Jesus did say he wanted to pass "the full measure of [his] joy" to those who believed in him (John 17:13).

We know Jesus gathered children around him, and with them, he laughed, smiled, and enjoyed life with a joy that comes only from trusting the Father like a little child: "See how very much our Father loves us, for he calls us his children, and that is what we are!" (1 John 3:1 NLT).

If we are always frowning and scowling, why are we surprised when the people around us have no interest in our Christian witness? Our objective-in-Jesus is to grow so intimate with the Father that we are able to show others the joyful and abundant life he gives.

LOVE NEEDS NO "BECAUSE"

*Very rarely will anyone die for a righteous man, though
for a good man someone might possibly dare to die.*
Romans 5:7

The love of God needs no "because." He does not give his love because of something you have done. He does not give his love because of something he will gain. He does not give his love because it is something you have earned.

God gives his love with no "because."

We give our love with conditions: "You can take it or leave it."

God gives his love with no conditions: "I'll take you and I won't leave you."

When we were still in rebellion against God's love, Jesus said, "I lay down my life ... No one takes it from me, but I lay it down of my own accord" (John 10:17 – 18).

I lay it down, Jesus says, with no need for "because."

And then he says, " 'I've given you an example; now do as I have done' " (John 13:15, author paraphrase). We too are to love as Jesus has loved.

OBJECTIVE-IN-JESUS: MATURITY

Therefore let us leave the elementary teachings
about Christ and go on to maturity.
Hebrews 6:1

Although God does the heavy lifting in our transformation into Christlike beings, we still bear the responsibility to keep discipline part of discipleship.

As Paul describes in 1 Corinthians 9, we beat our bodies into submission as we press on toward our objective-in-Jesus. But, as we're beating discipline into our thoughts and behavior, we too often beat ourselves up over our inability to do the things we ought to do (Romans 7:16–25).

Becoming like Jesus is difficult enough without this "Try harder!" mentality that sucks us into a cycle of I must, I ought, and I should, leaving us feeling defeated.

Paul says we are to push toward the ideal, but his standards never demand immediate perfection from us because he understands our desperate need for God's grace.

So, we make it our objective to mature into believers who think and act just like Jesus. We may slip, we may fall horribly, but we press on to take hold of the abundant life in Christ Jesus our Lord.

In Sync with God's Spirit

*"I in them and you in me. May they be brought to complete
unity to let the world know that you sent me and
have loved them even as you have loved me."*
John 17:23

Before you became a follower of Jesus, the spirit within you was dead in sin. But then, when you invited Jesus into your heart, God breathed new life into your spirit, making you a new creation in Christ.

Your soul is now anchored to his Spirit, a steadfast force working within you so you can choose not to be pushed about by events, circumstances, or even your feelings. Instead you can choose to let your life be controlled by the Spirit of God within you.

God wants you in sync with his Spirit in such a way that you are compelled to act as one with God, where his desires become your desires, where you chase after God's own heart.

The fact that God breathed his Spirit into you means you are never alone, and you are *never on your own* as you make decisions in faith.

A Better Place to Be

Pray to the LORD for it, because if it prospers,
you too will prosper.
Jeremiah 29:7

It is very possible that as you read this you are wishing you were somewhere else, living a different life.

God has a word for you; it's the same word he gave a group of people exiled from their homeland. Through the prophet Jeremiah, God told them, "You're not going home any time soon, so start making your lives here ... and pray for the peace and prosperity of the place where you're currently living because, by doing that, you too will be blessed with peace and prosperity" (Jeremiah 29:5 – 7, author paraphrase).

Our objective-in-Jesus is to no longer invest our energy in hopes of leaving, but instead to invest our energy in those around us. In other words, don't be physically present but mentally somewhere else, thinking of the future or the past, or thinking of someplace else. Our journey with Jesus requires we be fully present *in the present.*

You may feel like you are in exile, but God is working in ways you may not see. His message to you is: "Dig in and fully embrace the life around you."

STAY IN STEP WITH THE WOW!

*His divine power has given us everything we need for life
and godliness through our knowledge of him who
called us by his own glory and goodness.*
2 Peter 1:3

Christ Jesus lives in you today! The "wow!" is with you always and forever; yesterday, today, and tomorrow. Wow!

What does this mean?

Keep your heart and mind on the "wow!" Stay intentionally and consistently focused on the "wow!" "Set your hearts ... your minds on things above, not on earthly things" (Colossians 3:1–2).

Stay in step with the "wow!" The only way to the "wow!" is through Jesus, who is "the way and the truth and the life." We stay in step with the "wow!" when we stay in step with Jesus (John 14:6–7).

Understand no commandment is harmed. No commandment is harmed by focusing on the "wow!" "Love is the fulfillment of the law" (Romans 13:10).

The good news of the gospel is the "wow!" We proclaim without shame that the "wow!" is in our hearts.

Father, renew and maintain in us your steadfast spirit (Psalm 51:10). Shape us by your "wow!" and let it flow through us like living water from the eternal springs of heaven.

Love as an Active Verb

This is how God showed his love among us: He sent his one and only Son into the world that we might live through him.
1 John 4:9

Years ago my big sister was pregnant with her third child. At the very same time my girlfriend and I were faced with a crisis pregnancy. My sister offered to adopt our baby and raise it right along with hers: "Since the two babies are due almost at the same time, it would be like having twins."

She personified love as an active verb.

The foolishness of *speaking* love without *acting* love is illustrated by a famous *Peanuts* comic. Sally, Charlie Brown's little sister, stands inside a warm, dry house looking through a window at Snoopy, who sits on top of his doghouse freezing and wet in the snow.

Instead of inviting Snoopy into the house or caring for his comfort, Sally says to him, in effect, "Go in peace, keep warm, and eat well" (James 2:16 HCSB). Her words offer nice sentiments, but they don't mobilize hands and feet into service.

We love others by showing up in their broken lives and loving them sacrificially and unconditionally.

SIN AND SELF-CENTEREDNESS

Through these he has given us his very great and precious
promises, so that through them you may participate
in the divine nature and escape the corruption
in the world caused by evil desires.
2 Peter 1:4

Living for yourself is sin.

When we live for ourselves, we live as if we are separated from God, and that's when we become mean and selfish, insensitive and manipulative.

However, when we believe in Christ and receive him into our hearts, we become "partakers of the divine nature" (2 Peter 1:4 NASB). We become new creations (2 Corinthians 5:17), joined for eternity with God's life. This God-life is active in us as the Holy Spirit indwells our being.

By believing the *truth*—that God is looking out for us—we no longer need to look out for ourselves. Instead, we can look out for others (Matthew 6:33; Philippians 4:19).

Our objective-in-Jesus is to grow confident of the truth that God's life within us will guide us to the places we need to go. There we can lovingly meet the needs of others and become active in serving God.

YAHWEH CAUSES TO BE

*"I will cause all My goodness to pass in front of you,
and I will proclaim the name Yahweh before you."*
Exodus 33:19a (HCSB)

God knows you by name, and he wants you to know him by name.

Yahweh means "he causes to be." It is God's personal name, just like we attach our individuality with our first or last names.

"He causes to be" is a declaration by God that he is the creator of the universe. He created the planets and the stars, he created all there is in this world, and he created you and me. Yahweh has the juice to make things happen and the ability to show you compassion, by getting right into the mess with you, making good on every promise he has made.

Yahweh is not some "god-watching-from-a-distance"; Yahweh is beside you, and he's placed the Holy Spirit inside you.

How would your behavior change if you abandoned yourself to the belief that God cared for you deeply and forever? Ask God to show you the places in your life where you are a "person-at-a-distance" from God.

THE JESUS-DEPOSIT

You became imitators of us and of the Lord . . .
And so you became a model to all the believers.
1 Thessalonians 1:6–7

Think of this: the Great Commission is so vast, and your role is so critical, that God needs you to be in thousands of places at one time. You may be thinking, "But that's humanly impossible!"

Yet, God's strategy is so simple we might call it common sense. He puts a Jesus-deposit in you, and then guides you with his supernatural strength to just the right places at just the right time, to meet just the right people so you can teach them how to become living, breathing examples of Jesus.

And then, they tell and teach others, who tell and teach others, who tell and teach others. In this sense, you're now simultaneously all over the globe because "Christ in you" is now "Christ in others."

This is how the early church grew. The first Jesus-ones received the deposit of the Holy Spirit and then became models to all the believers—simultaneously their faith in God became known everywhere (1 Thessalonians 1:6–8).

The same Holy Spirit is at work in you, expanding your ability to minister beyond human possibilities.

THREE SHEEP DEEP

He said, "Lord, you know all things; you know that I love you."
Jesus said, "Feed my sheep."
John 21:17

Jesus asked, "Do you truly love me more than these?"

Peter looked toward the other disciples, whom he always considered second compared to his love and loyalty for Jesus: "Yes, Lord, you know that I love you."

Jesus said, "Feed my lambs," and echoing in Peter's head was the thought: "After you've been sifted, return to strengthen the brothers."

Again, Jesus asked, "Do you truly love me?"

Peter looked at Jesus, remembering that the last time their eyes had locked he'd denied even knowing the man: "Yes, Lord, you know that I love you."

Jesus said, "Take care of my sheep."

Finally, Jesus asked, "Do you love me?"

Peter cried, "Lord, you know all things; you know that I love you."

And Jesus said, "Feed my sheep" (John 21:15–17).

In your failure, hear Jesus whisper: "Get on with it. You've returned; you're restored. Now strengthen the others. Feed my sheep."

ENCOURAGED INTO COURAGE

We who are strong ought to bear with the failings
of the weak and not to please ourselves. Each of us
should please his neighbor for his good, to build him up.
Romans 15:1–2

Encouragement is part of God's nature, and we become godly encouragers when we "bear the weaknesses of those without strength" (Romans 15:1 NASB).

In this, we help build others toward a stronger faith, just as the Holy Spirit works within us to strengthen our faith.

We encourage others when we affirm them and then confirm God's work in their lives (1 Thessalonians 1:8–10). We encourage others when we support and reassure them during trials and tribulations (1 Thessalonians 5:14). We encourage others when we offer reconciliation and restoration to those straying from their faith (Galatians 6:1; James 5:19–20).

Our objective, then, is to grow in Christ until we are always on the lookout for those who need God's encouragement. When we encourage, we help others develop the courage needed to keep going when faced with failing faith, and to keep growing in Christ when God seems far away.

Negotiating Belief

What does the Scripture say? "Abraham believed God."
Romans 4:3

The apostle Paul, who received his sight when he became blind, says the cure for unbelief is, quite simply, to believe!

He makes his point with one phrase: "Abraham believed God" (Romans 4:3).

Abraham believed God would speak with him.

Abraham believed God would listen to him.

Abraham believed God knew more than he did when the childless patriarch was called to birth a great nation.

Abraham believed God was telling him to go, even if it was to a land he did not know (Hebrews 11:8).

Abraham leaned hard into his belief because he maintained an intimate friendship with the Father above. By staying close to God, Abraham grew confident that the Almighty could be trusted to do the things he said he would do and to fulfill the commitments he promised to complete.

Pray, "God, I do believe; help me overcome my unbelief!" (Mark 9:24).

LETTING GO OF OUR CONFIDENCE

For God is working in you, giving you the desire
and the power to do what pleases him.
Philippians 2:13 (NLT)

The secret to living with confidence is to become confident in God's unlimited compassion and power as we let go of our confidence in ourselves.

When we think we have to do it on our own, or when we think we *are* doing it on our own, we stand on an uncertain foundation, like the man who built his house upon the sand (Matthew 7:26–27). No matter how confident we are in ourselves, eventually the rains will come and wash away our self-confidence.

But when we have God-confidence, we know that God is with us always—even unto the ends of the earth, even when we open our mouths to speak, even in everything (Philippians 4:13).

You may be thinking, "There's something I'd really like to do, that I think God is telling me to do, but I don't think that I can do it." This kind of thinking will keep you from even trying, but if you are confident in God and what he can do through your life, you have every reason to move forward and no good reason to stand still.

GIVE LIFE WITH YOUR WORDS

The tongue has the power of life and death,
and those who love it will eat its fruit.
Proverbs 18:21

You have the power to kill or give life.

Yes, you, gentle reader—the one with Jesus in your heart—are capable of murder. And so am I.

We have the power to speak death with our words, and we have the power to speak life.

Perhaps you've been on the receiving end of a message meant to murder: "You're not smart enough. You're not thin enough. You're not fast enough. You're not good enough. A real Christian wouldn't think such a thing."

In a world where people are beat up and put down, God gives you superhero power to punch through the negativity. You speak life to others when you say: "You matter to me. I like you just the way you are. You're human, anyone could think that. Your life counts. You were created for a purpose. God loves you, and you're incredibly valuable to him."

You can become the voice of God's grace in the lives of others, supporting, loving, helping, and encouraging with the words that flow from your mouth (Romans 14:19).

SERVING WITH OUR PRESENCE

"Martha, Martha," the Lord answered, "you are worried
and upset about many things, but only one thing is needed.
Mary has chosen what is better, and it will not be
taken away from her."
Luke 10:41–42

Martha was busy for Jesus, and that left her *too busy to be with Jesus.*

Jesus was sitting in her living room, but she was in her kitchen steaming vegetables for God. Don't misunderstand; no doubt Jesus would be blessed by a hot meal served by the best cook in Bethany.

However, since Jesus always valued relationships over anything else, his preference might have been a simple cheese and olive pita in exchange for time spent enjoying Martha's company.

Jesus may have simply wanted to relax among friends. There is a sacramental element to serving others simply with our presence. Can you consider that Jesus may be blessed just to hang out with you?

We seek God first, and *then* we do the things he wants us to do. Nudge Mary over and sit down at the feet of Jesus. Find out what's on his mind.

CONFESSION:
GRACE, NOT DISGRACE

*Confess your sins to each other and pray for each other
so that you may be healed.*
James 5:16

Confession is about grace, not disgrace. Confession leads to restoration, not humiliation.

God forgives us even before we confess; our confession is simply agreeing with God that we've sinned. When we agree with God, he inhabits our healing. Like a sin-addict, the first step toward healing is admitting we have a problem — and that problem is rebellion against God.

Confession moves us back toward oneness with God. We agree we've returned to the ramparts of our own will and have broken with the safety of God's will. In confession, we are the prodigal running home to the open arms of the Father.

In response, the Father offers grace; he commands the dogs of disgrace to return to their caves, unable to gnaw on the bones of condemnation.

Confession reduces the power of secrets gathered in the far country. We reveal and God heals, liberating our souls from the chains that constrict our faith and distract us from this magnificent truth: We have the freedom to no longer sin, but instead, to make choices pleasing to God.

GOD'S HOLY SENTENCE

"So then, it was not you who sent me here, but God."
Genesis 45:8

In the story of your life, you are in the middle of a sentence today. You may find yourself paused in a painful place, something Steve Pettit calls the holy "but God" in a sentence.

You find this divine "but God" structured into sentences throughout the Bible:

Joseph's brothers sold him into slavery, but God used it to preserve the Jewish race.

The Israelites were enslaved in Egypt, but God sent Moses to lead them to the Promised Land.

Jesus died on a cross, but God used that very moment to deliver us all from the evil one.

There will be many days when we wonder what God is doing, *but* God will do something unexpected and marvelous. We don't know what's behind the "but God"; yet, we can grow in confidence that God is in the sentence with us and he is working toward exactly the best thing he can provide for us.

How Can I Forgive That?

In him we have redemption through his blood, the forgiveness
of sins, in accordance with the riches of God's grace that he
lavished on us with all wisdom and understanding.
Ephesians 1:7–8

The more we feel hurt, the more likely we are to cling to the idea that forgiveness is dependent on how much the one who offended us grovels in guilt. This makes it easier to say, "I can't forgive him until he learns his lesson," or "If I forgive her, then she'll get away with it."

Yet the Bible teaches forgiveness is an unconditional offering of grace.

When you forgive, it doesn't mean the person who hurt you won't have to face any consequences. You can forgive someone who has committed a criminal offense against you, but he still may have to face prosecution, a jail sentence, or the possibility of paying restitution.

God forgives you even before you ask for it, and he calls you to forgive others before they ask for it — even before they show signs of remorse. When we forgive, we are free to see how "God causes everything to work together for the good of those who love God and are called according to his purpose for them" (Romans 8:28 NLT).

IS JESUS CAPABLE?

*For he has rescued us from the dominion of darkness and
brought us into the kingdom of the Son he loves.*
Colossians 1:13

When Jesus pours his Spirit into our hearts, it represents a
change of leadership. Before this Jesus-event, we are in charge,
making decisions independent of God. After the Spirit's infu-
sion, God is in charge and we make decisions dependent on
him. We confess, "I can't; God can."

Paul describes this change in leadership as a transfer
from the Devil's domain of darkness into God's "kingdom
of the Son he loves." In one realm, the Devil is the despot; in
the other, Jesus rules with love, redemption, and forgiveness
(Matthew 11:30; Luke 24:47).

When this transfer takes place, we face a choice: Will we
submit to God's leadership or will we continue to make decisions based on how we did it when we were aligned with the
renegade regime?

When we continue to make decisions independent of
Jesus—decisions without faith—then we are essentially saying Jesus is incapable of managing our lives. If you believe
Jesus is capable, ask God to show you why you are unwilling
or unable to rest in that truth (Mark 9:24).

GOD PRESSES US TOWARD TRUST

We are hard pressed on every side, but not crushed.
2 Corinthians 4:8

Our older brother Paul says we can rest assured that our hardships are not meant to defeat us. We may be hard pressed, yet our hope in God keeps us from being crushed; perplexed, yet our hope in God keeps us from despair; persecuted, yet our hope in God tells us we're not abandoned; struck down, yet our God keeps us from being destroyed (2 Corinthians 4:8–9).

Like jars of clay, chipped and blemished, we are fragile by design so that the glorious light of God will shine through our cracks and crevices.

When someone looks at us, they should be able to say, "What's this? That plain jar of clay couldn't possibly be creating such a glorious light; it must be the light of heaven contained within. The peace and joy and love I see in that light must be from God."

God's plan is that every time we face these hardships, we are pressed, bit by bit, into the truth that God alone is our strength and the weight we carry is not our burden alone. And in our weakness and exhaustion, in our frustrations and our failures, in our anger and our pain, God's light shines through.

EQUIPPED

May the God of peace ... equip you with everything good for doing his will.
Hebrews 13:20–21

God gives you everything you need to succeed in your Jesus-life.

The writer of Hebrews refers to this as equipping, and it is similar to providing a sports team with the necessary training and equipment to succeed.

The Bible says God will not just provide you with the material things you need; he will also become your strength, your wisdom, and your guidance. He will open doors of support and close doors that will take you in the wrong direction.

God equips you through others. One way God will equip you is through your family, friends, and coworkers. There are many ways they can support you, but the *most important* thing they can do is model a Jesus-life for you and help you bring your fears, concerns, and struggles into the light, so God can move you into a faith that abandons all fears.

God equips others through you. The Jesus-life in you can help others see God as an encourager and a supporter, and Jesus as a loving "friend who sticks closer than a brother" (Proverbs 18:24).

JESUS STOPPED

Jesus stopped and ordered the man to be brought to him.
When he came near, Jesus asked him,
"What do you want me to do for you?"
"Lord, I want to see," he replied.
Luke 18:40–41

Jesus stopped. He stopped when people needed his help, when they needed his comfort, when they needed his protection, when they needed an answer to a perplexing problem.

Jesus saw the interruptions in his life as divine opportunities to show God's love to people in desperate need.

Jesus expressed love through action, and we are called to do the same. Woe to those who become so busy saving the world that they are unable to stop when they see someone in need in their own backyard.

John, the apostle of love, explained it like this: "If you see some brother or sister in need and have the means to do something about it but turn a cold shoulder and do nothing, what happens to God's love? It disappears. *And you made it disappear*" (1 John 3:17 MSG, emphasis added).

For Jesus, love is a show-*then*-tell activity. Our objective-in-Jesus is to stop and show our love, knowing that it will tell others we love them.

TRUTH: GOD USES MY MISTAKES FOR HIS GLORY

Therefore I will boast all the more gladly about my weaknesses,
so that Christ's power may rest on me.
2 Corinthians 12:9

In faith, *I know this to be true*: God takes my mistakes and uses them for his glory.

After Joseph's brothers sold him into slavery, he told them later, "But God sent me ahead of you to preserve for you a remnant on earth and to save your lives by a great deliverance" (Genesis 45:7).

God took the brothers' self-centered action, motivated by jealousy and anger, and worked it into his plan of redemption (Genesis 45).

I know it is true that God can take my sins and mistakes and he can use them for good.

Jesus said, "Simon, Simon, Satan has asked to sift you as wheat" (Luke 22:31). But when Peter failed, Jesus knew he'd reached the point of, "I can't, but God can," and Jesus said, "Feed my sheep" (John 21:17).

I know it is true that God will still use me in ministry, even after I sin or make mistakes.

DO THE INTERESTS OF JESUS
INTEREST YOU?

And whatever you do, whether in word or deed,
do it all in the name of the Lord Jesus.
Colossians 3:17

When you became a believer, your role in life changed. You no longer have the job of looking out for your own interests; your job now is to represent the interests of Jesus.

You are the face of Jesus, showing up in the lives of others on his behalf. You show up in hospitals; you show up at funerals; you show up at weddings; you show up across the table as you share coffee with a friend.

You show up in hospitals; you show up at funerals; you show up at weddings; you show up across the dinner table; and you show up over coffee with a friend. No matter what action you take — whether it's something you say or something you do — you are on the job for Jesus (Colossians 3:17).

The more you serve others in love, the more you'll be able to influence them toward faith in Jesus Christ. The apostle Paul wrote, "Though I am free and belong to no man, I make myself a slave to everyone, to win as many as possible" (1 Corinthians 9:19).

THE PIG JUST ASKED
FOR SOME BISCUITS

*"Father, I have sinned against heaven and against you.
I am no longer worthy to be called your son."*
Luke 15:18 – 19

While sitting among pigs, the prodigal son finally sees himself as wretched. There's nothing like having a pig ask you to pass the biscuits to help you see you really are in a mess.

Rabbi Paul says we've got to get to *wretched* status so we can see we need a Savior: "Who will rescue me from this body of death?" (Romans 7:24).

The prodigal's father lets him wander off to the far country, just like God gives us the freedom to wallow with pigs, if we are destructively dense enough to do so.

If you are sitting with the pigs, consider God is pushing you toward the moment when you see yourself as wretched; see your sin as wretched; see your life as wretched; so you can, then, move on to see the One who will rescue you from this cycle of defeat. God will wash the pig smell away with the hyssop of Christ's blood (Psalm 51:7).

GOD, WE ARE LOOKING TO YOU

*"O LORD, God of Israel ... you alone are God
over all the kingdoms of the earth."*
2 Kings 19:15

Surrounded by 185,000 enemy troops, who had never lost a battle in their conquest of the world, King Hezekiah listened to a message that, in essence, said, "Surrender and we'll let your people live as slaves. Otherwise, we're coming in to kill you all."

With nowhere else to turn, Hezekiah took the matter to God. He sought God first, in worship, before asking for anything. Then, almost as an afterthought, Hezekiah said, "Oh yeah, there's this big army outside. God, we don't know what to do, so we're looking to you."

When we maximize our problems, we minimize God's greatness and we also minimize — *in our minds* — God's ability to handle our problems.

Hezekiah acknowledged and maximized God's sovereignty and power over the facts of the situation, and that lifted the crisis above mere human thinking.

The next morning, Hezekiah looked out across the enemy encampments and he saw the invading army laid waste by an angel of God (2 Kings 19:35). *God, we don't know what to do, so we're looking to you.*

A FATHER HEART: LOVE AND OBEY

"If you love me, you will obey what I command."
John 14:15

Jesus said you show your love for him when you do what he tells you to do.

This doesn't mean you love him out of obligation. That's the quickest way to destroy love. The Bible teaches love is not demanding (1 Corinthians 13:5 NLT).

Rather, because you love Jesus, you care about the things that matter to him. You become one with the will of Jesus, and his will is to always do what the Father tells him to do. In this way, you become one with Jesus and one with your heavenly Father.

This oneness is reinforced by the Holy Spirit working within us, connecting us to God and to other believers. The more you obey God in the details of your life, the more real he becomes to you as you see the intimate practicality he brings to your relationship. You begin to see, day in and day out, that God faithfully levels the path before you and covers the path you leave behind.

And, through this, you learn to love God "with all your heart, soul, strength, and mind" (Luke 10:27 CEV).

NOT *YOUR* WILL, BUT MINE?

"My Father, if it is possible, may this cup be taken from me.
Yet not as I will, but as you will."
Matthew 26:39

In our clash of wills with God, we are tempted to pray, "My will, not yours."

But that is a prayer of separation and division. It's the invocation in a worship service of one; the prayer request that brings Christian growth to a slam-on-the-brakes halt.

Jesus prayed, "Not my will, but yours." It is easy to forget he still prays that prayer today, by the Spirit groaning within us when we don't yet know the words to say.

When we say, "Amen and so be it," we become one with God's will, joining him as he loves others through us. In our abandonment to the Father's will, we put ourselves aside in order to "help others get ahead" (Philippians 2:3 MSG).

The life of God flowed through Jesus because he emptied himself of all personal concerns for comfort and honor; he demonstrated for all time that God's power isn't found in seizing and grasping and taking, but in emptying and being spent for others.

You enter that God-life by praying, "Not as I will, Father, but as you will."

WHAT DO YOUR
COMMITMENTS SAY?

*They gave themselves first to the Lord and then to us
in keeping with God's will.*
2 Corinthians 8:5

God created us to make and stay in commitments, starting first with our commitment to him and then with our commitment to others.

Staying committed to one another takes time, and it requires we live life together beyond the walls of the worship center. It means we make others a priority by living with them—over coffee, after work, at the ballpark, in the hospital. It means making the frightening move beyond superficial friendships toward becoming friends who stick together closer than brothers and sisters (Proverbs 18:24).

But it all starts with God: As we deepen our relationship with God, he compels us to deepen our relationships with others.

Although we're not able to develop deep commitments with everyone, God did design us to have at least a few deep commitments with others in the Jesus-body.

If you haven't already, make an intentional commitment to one other Jesus-one, saying, "I want you to know that I will always be there for you."

PLAYING SECOND FIDDLE

*Therefore ... offer your bodies as living sacrifices, holy and
pleasing to God—this is your spiritual act of worship.*
Romans 12:1

Paul says when we honor others over ourselves, we please
and worship God. We become "living sacrifices" as we move
from self-centeredness to other-centeredness. Eugene Peterson
paraphrases Paul like this: "Be good friends who love deeply;
practice playing second fiddle" (Romans 12:10 MSG).

And so it goes that I was jockeying to be next in line at a
fast-food restaurant, but as I grabbed for the door, the words
"Practice playing second fiddle" came to me and God spoke
into my thoughts: "What does it matter in eternity if you
get a burger thirty-five seconds later than someone else?" I
stopped and let the people behind me enter first.

Allowing others to go before me when I was in a rush
went against my natural inclinations, but God told me to
sacrifice my inclinations on his altar.

And so that moment became an act of worship. You can
worship God today by the things you do and by the way you
do them, no matter how insignificant they seem.

GRACE, GRACE, GRACE

If his good deeds had made him acceptable to God,
he would have had something to boast about.
But that was not God's way.
Romans 4:2 (NLT)

If, after reading these devotions, you carry away only one thing, my prayer is that it will be a mind-transforming, behavior-altering understanding of God's infinite, indestructible, and immovable grace.

Don't just take a quick, yet correct, sound-bite explanation like "grace is the unmerited favor of God." Understand the ancient, eternal meaning of grace that stretches across the depth and breadth and width and height of God's character.

These devotionals present a high standard for Christian discipleship. My hope is to press us both—myself as well as you—toward an honest assessment of our faith, a deeper commitment to our beliefs, and—most importantly—a sacrificial, wholly abandoned love for the Lord Jesus Christ.

Yes, the standard is high. Truth says it's impossibly high. That's why we need God's grace. We cannot do it, but God can and will do it if we let him rule our lives. Our objective-in-Jesus is to develop the confidence that our competence comes from God (2 Corinthians 3:4–5).

Your Weakness, God's Glory

But we have this treasure in jars of clay to show that this all-surpassing power is from God and not from us.

2 Corinthians 4:7

We stand as monuments of God's grace, and we bear an inscription written in God's own hand: "Within this earthen container, the One True God is at work."

This is why our older brother, Paul, says we can boast about our weaknesses; because where we are weak, God is able to show up even stronger as his "all-surpassing power" shines even brighter from within our fractured and shattered lives.

Your weaknesses are a gift. God designed you with your weaknesses; they didn't just show up, surprising even God. He placed them very deliberately into his blueprint for you, which is why we all have different weaknesses and different strengths. God uses your weaknesses to bring you closer to him, so he can then bring you closer to the image of Jesus.

You don't have to look good. So, stop trying! Just be who you are, a frail human designed by God to reveal his glory. Truthfully, we could use a whole lot more authenticity in the church. If you're hurt, say it; if you're angry, admit it; if you're in love, show it; if you're wrong, confess it; if you're in need, reveal it.

WE ARE DESPERATE FOR YOU

Answer me when I call, O God of my righteousness!
You have relieved me in my distress;
Be gracious to me and hear my prayer.
Psalm 4:1 (NASB)

Lord, we are desperate for you. We are bunched up in confusion, moving by impulse and fear, flitting here and there like a frenzied flock caught in the wilderness of the far country.

We are here! We are here! And we know you *hear*; you have heard us before; you have swept in like shock and awe and saved us from our hopeless paralysis.

Do it again, O Holy One; how long must we wait?

And we hear you say, "Yes, how long? How long must I wait while you wear my grace and peace like a cheap cloak from a secondhand store?"

O God, I hear your heart. You set me apart, yet I joined the crowd — like birds of a feather.

From now on, Abba, when the swirl and twirl shoves at me, instead of taking to panicked wings, I will let you quiet my soul.

I am ready now; I am willing now to be swept under the safety of your wings, "as a hen gathers her chicks" (Matthew 23:37 NKJV).

COMPASSION IS AS
COMPASSION DOES

On one occasion an expert in the law stood up to test Jesus.
"Teacher," he asked, "what must I do to inherit eternal life?"
Luke 10:25

After teaching that the greatest commandment is "Love the Lord your God," Jesus added that the second greatest commandment is "Love your neighbor as yourself" (Luke 10:27). But then a lawyer asked Jesus, "Who is my neighbor?" (Luke 10:29).

Jesus, a gentle teacher with a gentle yoke, did not answer directly. Instead, he told a story about a man beaten and left for dead on the road to Jericho.

When a priest, and then a manager from the local temple, saw the injured man, they quickly crossed to the other side of the road.

But then a man from a despised race, a Samaritan, stopped. He treated the man's injuries and took him to a nearby inn, paying for the injured man's care and lodging until he could get back on his feet.

Who, Jesus asked, was the injured man's neighbor?

The lawyer responded, "The one who showed him mercy."

"That's right," Jesus said, "Now go and do the same" (Luke 10:37, based on NLT).

DIRECTLY CONNECTED WITH GOD

God has chosen to make known among the Gentiles
the glorious riches of this mystery,
which is Christ in you, the hope of glory.
Colossians 1:27

While moving through the line in a college cafeteria, my friend spotted a note next to a bowl of apples: "Please take only one apple. Remember, God is watching!"

With his one apple in hand, my friend got to the end of the line and saw another note next to a bowl of cookies. This one was hand-written: "Take all the cookies you want! God is watching the apples."

It's a comic absurdity, the way we behave as if there are parts of our lives that remain separated from God's omnipresent Spirit. The brutal and bloody truth is that the death of Jesus released the Holy Spirit to dwell within you.

As a believer, you are now united with Jesus. "Christ in you" doesn't mean you are divine; rather, it means you are directly connected with the divine nature (Colossians 1:27; 2 Peter 1:3–4). This enables you to live an authentic God-life, and to live it abundantly (John 4:14; 10:10).

COOPERATING WITH A SMILE

Whatever you do, work at it with all your heart,
as working for the Lord, not for men.
Colossians 3:23

Years ago I worked for someone I didn't respect. I would do whatever this boss asked of me, but I tended to drag my feet and complain.

Yet, God used the relationship to teach me godly obedience to my earthly authorities. He spoke to me through a plaque my boss kept on his desk: "Cooperation is doing with a smile what you have to do anyway."

You won't find that sentence in the Bible, but it sums up our need to be obedient to God's commands, regardless of what we think or feel in the moment.

God used that sign to change my attitude. Then he led me to seek forgiveness from my boss for my disrespect. It was a major turning point in my life, teaching me what it meant to be a man under authority, *regardless of who was in authority*.

And you know what? As I responded to God's direction through my earthly employer, I developed considerable respect for my boss and he became one of my greatest mentors and supporters. Make it your objective-in-Jesus to cooperate with a smile.

My Desire Is One with You

Dear friends, if our hearts do not condemn us, we have
confidence before God and receive from him anything we ask,
because we obey his commands and do what pleases him.
1 John 3:21–22

Father, my desire is one with your desire. I want to maintain a clear conscience and a pure heart, and I admit I can't do it without your power at work in me.

I see now that when I'm not moving toward oneness with your desires, then I'm moving toward oneness with the enemy's desires.

It's impossible to be loyal to you while also maintaining loyalty to ungodly habits, improper thoughts, and belief in my own independence (Matthew 6:24). Those things, intentional or not, move me toward loyalty with the enemy, who is at war with you.

Invade my beliefs and overthrow any that are hollow, flimsy imitations of belief in you. Pull down and uproot any false beliefs that suggest I can't trust you.

Run free within me, Yahweh, so that my heart begins to beat with yours, and I am changed deep from my inside all the way to my outside, committed to you from head to toe.

THE INVASION OF PEACE

And those who are peacemakers will plant seeds of peace
and reap a harvest of righteousness.
James 3:18 (NLT)

A peacemaker is not the same as a peacekeeper.

The critical difference is this: The peacekeeper seeks to keep the peace by maintaining a delicate balance between factions who are in conflict; the peacemaker seeks to create peace by invading the conflict with love.

Jesus is a peacemaker. He enters our conflict with God, bringing an aggressive love that simply will not stop until we make peace with God.

We too are called to be peacemakers, helping others make peace with God, and then helping them make peace with each other. We do this by entering their lives with an aggressive love that flows from God's heart through ours.

Our peace-filled invasion is based on faith: "Therefore, since we have been justified through faith, we have peace with God through our Lord Jesus Christ" (Romans 5:1).

So we proclaim that peace with God comes through an unconditional surrender. Yet God, benevolent in victory, will say, "Go in peace and be freed from your suffering" (Mark 5:34).

Gracious Uncertainty

"I tell you the truth, unless you change and become like little children, you will never enter the kingdom of heaven."
Matthew 18:3

When my son first started playing baseball, it wasn't uncommon for him to ask, "Is my game today?" He wasn't questioning if something would happen; it was a given that it would. Instead, he was dependent on my wife or me to tell him when it would happen.

Oswald Chambers, in *My Utmost for His Highest*, describes this as "gracious uncertainty," where "we are uncertain of the next step, but we are certain of God."

With gracious uncertainty, we can be confident in our expectations, knowing our hope in the Lord will not disappoint us (Romans 5:5); we can release the things we have no responsibility for, yet worry about anyway.

My son can be certain I will get him to the ball game, trusting I have a handle on the details and I'll let him know when it is time to go.

We should have such faith: Make it your objective to grow confident that your heavenly Father will come through at just the right time in just the right way.

GUILT OFFERINGS

But go and learn what this means:
"I desire mercy, not sacrifice."
Matthew 9:13

He cradled the roses in his left arm like a running back carries a football. They'd cost him plenty, but that's the price you have to pay when you let someone down. Today was their anniversary—which he forgot.

Forgot because he was under pressure at work to complete a project; forgot because he needed to do well, not just because of ambition, but because he needed a promotion. The money was tight, and he wanted to be able to support his family in a better way.

The roses were a huge expense, but it was a necessary sacrifice to make it up to his wife and to make him feel better about his guilt.

Now the image dissolves, and you see you are the one carrying the roses and you are bringing them to Jesus. The roses represent your "sacrifice," those things you do in an effort to make up for your bad behavior, to suck-up to God after you've sinned.

But Jesus says he doesn't want the roses; his desire is to give you mercy, not demand some sort of guilt offering.

OBJECTIVE-IN-JESUS: COURTESY

Each of us will give an account of himself to God.
Therefore let us stop passing judgment on one another.
Instead, make up your mind not to put any
stumbling block in ... your brother's way.
Romans 14:12–13

Our objective-in-Jesus is to maintain courtesy and respect, even when we disagree with one another.

Jesus teaches us to respond to rudeness, or even heart-deep evil, with kindness. Paul says we are to use the spiritual weapon of courtesy motivated by good: "Don't let evil get the best of you; get the best of evil by doing good" (Romans 12:21 MSG).

Paul also says that God does not see reactions, but only actions. We are responsible for our own behavior, our own choice of response: "Each of us will give an account of himself to God. Therefore let us stop passing judgment on one another" (Romans 14:12–13).

This echoes Jesus, when he says: "Why do you look at the speck of sawdust in your brother's eye and pay no attention to the plank in your own eye?" (Matthew 7:3).

Your courtesy carries the same strength as a gentle answer, which turns away anger and rudeness (Proverbs 15:1).

TRUTH IS JESUS

"I am the way and the truth and the life.
No one comes to the Father except through me."
John 14:6

The enemy's great lie is that we must remain separate from the Father. He uses smoke and mirrors to keep us from seeing that we are a new creation, enticing us to think and choose as though we are disconnected from Christ and each other.

To counter these lies, we must constantly stay intimate with the Truth. Our relationship to the truth is just that—a relationship with God's own Truth, the only begotten Son, the author and perfecter of our faith.

"Jesus, I accept that the truth is not based on my ability to understand your plans or all of who you are; the truth is not dependent on my thoughts and opinions because then they would be independent of you. What you say is the truth; what you think is the truth; what you do is the truth.

"You are the Truth and you're calling me to live with truth, know the truth, trust the truth, and act according to the truth. All glory and praise to you, forever and ever, amen."

WITH GREAT POWER COMES GREAT RESPONSIBILITY

Now to each one the manifestation of the Spirit
is given for the common good.
1 Corinthians 12:7

My son's middle school once had a Reward Day assembly, where students were given some really cool stuff.

At one point, a teacher put all the students' names into a huge bucket in order to draw one name for the biggest prize of all!

"I know you're only supposed to use special powers for good," my son said. "But if I had special powers, I would've been tempted to stop time just before the teacher called out the winner. And I would have gone up and put my own name in her hand."

My first thought was, "Wow, that really would be cool!" But, trying to be a responsible parent, what I said *out loud* was, "Yes, we should only use special powers for the good of others."

But then I started thinking, as Jesus-ones, *we do have a special power* planted deep within us — the Holy Spirit. The apostle Paul says we have been given this special power for the common good. And, as that great theologian Spiderman says: "With great power comes great responsibility."

LET GOD INTERPRET THE FACTS

When we heard this, we and the people there pleaded with Paul not to go up to Jerusalem.
Acts 21:12

When Paul's friends heard he would be arrested in Jerusalem, they immediately tried to talk him out of going, interpreting the facts from their limited perspective.

Yet, the whole truth is that Paul's arrest became the means God used to get him to Rome. Under house arrest, Paul began to write letters to the congregations he'd started, and those letters became a major part of the New Testament.

Paul also brought his ministry to the congregation in Rome and the Christ-followers there became a major influence in spreading the Gospel around the world.

It is a fact that Paul was arrested in Jerusalem, but God's interpretation of the circumstances was far different from Paul's friends.

Knowing the facts does not mean we know the truth about our circumstances. Our objective-in-Jesus is to trust God and leave it up to him to interpret facts.

JESUS STAYED
WITH GOD'S TIMETABLE

When he had received the drink, Jesus said, "It is finished."
With that, he bowed his head and gave up his spirit.
John 19:30

Timing was important to Jesus; everything in its time at just the right time. On a mission to radically transform humankind, he never rushed or struggled to play catch up.

As he walked through the New Testament, Jesus clearly worked using a different clock than everyone else. He never arrived late and he never arrived early; he arrived according to purpose.

Jesus was born at exactly the right time to be in Bethlehem with his parents, right as the stars aligned to announce the birth of Israel's long-awaited king.

Others thought he was late, but he arrived just in time to raise Lazarus from the dead.

Timing was so critical to Jesus and his mission that he even died right on time, finished in time to fulfill the prophecy that none of his bones would be broken.

God-timing means you say no to the urgent in order to stay focused on the things that matter in eternity.

The Involuntary Volunteer

*"If anyone would come after me, he must deny himself
and take up his cross daily and follow me."*
Luke 9:23

It's a classic comedy riff. A leader stands before a group and says, "I need a volunteer. There's little chance of success and most likely you'll die, but if you're willing to do it, take one step forward."

Everyone in the group looks around, and then they all take a step backward, except for one hapless bullwinkle who now appears to have taken a step forward. He's become an *involuntary* volunteer.

By its very nature, sacrificial service must be voluntary. Jesus, as a *voluntary* volunteer, says no one took his life from him, rather he gave it up freely: "I lay it down of my own accord. I have authority to lay it down and authority to take it up again. This command I received from my Father" (John 10:18).

In matters of sacrificial service, are we often among those who take a step backward, leaving others to *involuntarily* volunteer?

Our objective-in-Jesus is to step forward, offering to take the place of others, in particular those who are involuntary volunteers.

LOST ON THE SIN TRAIL

*You have been set free from sin
and have become slaves to righteousness.*

Romans 6:18

For years I wandered away from God. My image of that time is that of a traveler on a trail through the wilderness.

Wandering in the wilderness, I lost the memory that I was there because of my own sinful choices. Eventually, I lost the truth that I had any choice at all. I felt like I was held hostage by my choices and could only keep making the same ones over and over again.

Once I returned to God's path, I could clearly see I still had choices: I could continue down God's path; I could sit and mourn the waste; or I could return to my wanderings.

Most of all, I could *choose* not to sin. I am free from sin, not free from temptation, but free from the slavery of sin that kept me chained to ungodly choices.

Jesus broke the power of sin in your life, and he has empowered you, through the Holy Spirit, to make right, corrective, godly choices.

THE JOY OF CRUSHED BONES

Let me hear joy and gladness;
let the bones you have crushed rejoice.
Psalm 51:8

Brokenness is a good thing. Here's why: It's impossible to become intimate with God unless we are broken of our independence, broken of our pride, and broken of our insistence that our way is better than God's.

Brokenness is the prodigal fighting with pigs over food (Luke 15:11–32).

Brokenness is Jonah's acceptance of death to calm the storm, confessing the consequences of running from God, "I know that it is my fault that this great storm has come upon you" (Jonah 1:12).

Brokenness is Peter's weeping bitterly outside the trial of Jesus (Luke 22:62).

Like Jesus serving bread at the Last Supper, God takes us, breaks us, blesses us, and then uses us.

O Lord, may you hear our joy and gladness; may the bones you have crushed rejoice.

DOING WHAT GOD IS THINKING

"For who has known the mind of the Lord that he may instruct him?" But we have the mind of Christ.
1 Corinthians 2:16

In a land not so far away and a time not too distant, lived a mighty, yet gentle Master of the Manor. He had a servant of excellent efficiency, incorruptible integrity, and joyful heart.

But the Master also noticed the servant would do things, well-intentioned, yet not in line with his own wishes.

One day the Master was in his library, and he couldn't find one of his favorite books. Looking closely, he realized his entire library had been rearranged.

"Good servant, I did not ask you to rearrange the library," said the Master. "However, I did ask you to prepare the banquet hall for the guests we will receive tonight."

"Yes, Master," said the servant. "But I don't see anyone coming up the road, so I assumed the guests wouldn't actually arrive tonight."

With a tone of command coming into his voice, the Master said, "You serve me best when you begin to think as I think, instead of insisting I think like you."

Just then, the doorbell rang. The guests had arrived.

PARABLES OF GOD'S GRACE

Join with others in following my example, brothers, and take note of those who live according to the pattern we gave you.
Philippians 3:17

Sometimes when people ask me what I do for a living, I tell them I'm a professional observer. That's what writers do; we observe.

The truth is we are all observers; it's one of the ways we learn. Paul understood this and so he said if you want to see what a Jesus-one looks like, observe me and "those who live according to the pattern we gave you" (Philippians 3:17).

Modern research affirms Paul's insight into human nature. It's estimated that only about ten percent of us are able to take abstract ideas and produce tangible results without some sort of "hands-on" model.

Words may be important to share certain concepts, but we don't grow together by sharing words alone; we grow together by sharing life.

We see Jesus purposefully investing in the lives of others. When we make it our objective-in-Jesus to share life with others, they are able to observe an example of how God reproduces himself in and through us. We become living parables of God's grace.

GOD'S DANCE OF REDEMPTION

Let us fix our eyes on Jesus, the author and perfecter of our faith, who for the joy set before him endured the cross, scorning its shame, and sat down at the right hand of the throne of God.
Hebrews 12:2

The God-adventure is a sweeping dance of redemption, as he moves through history coordinating circumstances and events in order to bring as many people as possible home to heaven.

God, writing *his story*, keeps all things moving toward a purpose, a climax in history. His children follow him in faith, yet even the most faithful stumble and fail. But the story doesn't end there! God redeems even the worst mistakes, making all things work together for the good of those he calls his own.

God's story is a story of majesty, power, and infinite grace; it's about a God who speaks the world into existence and sets the moon and the stars in place, yet who also cares for every detail of your life.

God rescued you from captivity, and now he wants you to join him in further rescue missions, bringing more of his children—your brothers and sisters—home to the Father's house.

CRANKY CHRISTIANS UNITE!

I appeal to you ... in the name of our Lord Jesus Christ,
that all of you agree with one another so that there may be
no divisions among you and that you may be perfectly
united in mind and thought.
1 Corinthians 1:10

There is only one way a bunch of cranky Christians can be perfectly united in mind and thought, and that's if we each have the same access to the perfect mind of Jesus. The closer each of us moves toward Jesus, the closer we move toward each other.

God calls us to a higher standard than just getting along. We are to become one with each other, in mind and thought.

The difficulties we face in getting along with one another are meant to expose the areas where we still need to work on our Jesus-like character.

Even though we have differing opinions, in Christ we can agree on one thing: Jesus is the head, the mind, and his thoughts are the only ones that matter in the end (James 4:7). As we submit to the mind of Christ and walk in oneness with him, Jesus pulls us past our divisions and disputes with love that flows from the very fountain of God.

SNATCHING FROM GOD'S HAND

*We have renounced secret and shameful ways; we do not use
deception, nor do we distort the word of God.*
2 Corinthians 4:2

With a quick glance, it's easy to assume Paul is referring to the sinful behavior that occurred before we became
Christians. We *announce* our dependence on Jesus and we
renounce the sinful methods we once used to make it through
a Jesus-less day.

However, Paul is actually referring to the sinful behavior
of a group of Christians who slander him even as they manip-
ulate young believers. Paul ignores their specific attacks, calling us to press toward greater maturity, where we:

No longer act like children. Unlike a child, we are to stop
snatching situations out of his hands, thinking we can do
it better or faster. Because we are maturing in Jesus, we no
longer depend on secrecy, deception, or self-righteousness to
get our own way.

Trust that God can. Paul, ever the exhorter, pushes us
toward the ideal, but his standards are never imperative
"ought to" statements demanding perfection from us. He,
perhaps more than any other student in the school of Christ,
understands our desperate need for God's grace. We cannot
—God can. Our objective-in-Jesus is to trust God can.

BLESSINGS IN BLOOM

And what more shall I say? I do not have time to tell about Gideon, Barak, Samson, Jephthah, David, Samuel and the prophets.
Hebrews 11:32

Our objective-in-Jesus is to just gather facts, but leave it up to God to interpret them.

Sarai's interpretation of the facts assumed no one her age could conceive a child; God saw the whole truth, that her womb would bear many heirs (Genesis 15–21).

Gideon assumed he needed more men in order to succeed with God's plan; God saw the whole truth that three hundred men were sufficient (Judges 7).

The disciples assumed there wasn't enough food to feed the five thousand; Jesus, the Truth, saw enough food to include twelve baskets of leftovers (Mark 8:17–19).

Walking by faith means you trust God even in the most difficult of situations, even when things appear hopeless. He is the only One who sees the whole truth, who can transform all things into something good (Jeremiah 29:11; Romans 8:28).

Our objective-in-Jesus is to wait upon the Lord as we watch him turn what we assume to be disaster into a blessing.

FEARLESS LOVE

No one has ever seen God; but if we love one another,
God lives in us and his love is made complete in us.
1 John 4:12

God loves us; we love others. God gives to us; we give to others. This is the holy cycle initiated by the God who is love. He first loved us and, by his love within us, we can now love one another.

"God lives in us and his love is made complete in us" because, as it moves through us and into others, God's love comes full circle. Waves of his "perfect love" flood our lives (1 John 4:18), sweeping away the fears we've harbored in our hearts—fears of rejection, judgment, loneliness, unfairness, even death.

We no longer live in fear because "fear has to do with punishment," and we now know, through the love of God and the blood of Jesus, that our sins are forgiven. We give God our fears and he redeems them with love (1 John 4:18).

In turn, through this holy cycle of love we are enabled to love the fear out of one another as we live in Christ-community.

I'll Catch Up with You

*"You go to the Feast. I am not yet going up to this Feast,
because for me the right time has not yet come."*
John 7:8

You never think of Jesus as a hurried person. He never
seemed stressed over getting more things done. So when his
brothers said, "You ought to leave here and go to Judea ... No
one who wants to become a public figure acts in secret" (John
7:3–4), Jesus told them the timing wasn't right. The Father
hadn't told him to go yet.

As it was, Jesus followed almost immediately on the heels
of his brothers. But he went when God said to go, keeping him
from being swept into events that might distract him from his
purpose or that might push him off God's timetable.

Time after time, as Jesus walks through the Gospels, we
hear him referring to the Father's will; he knew he'd been sent
by God for a purpose, and he stuck to that purpose.

What's the best way to manage your time? Figure out
who God created you to be and what he created you to do,
and then resolutely set out to accomplish God's purpose
(Luke 9:51).

MOTIVATED BY VISION

Because the Lamb who is at the center of the throne will shepherd them; He will guide them to springs of living waters, and God will wipe away every tear from their eyes.
Revelation 7:17

An Olympic swimmer endures the long hours of staring at the bottom of a pool, day after day, because he holds a vision of the gold to come.

A mother endures the painful labor of childbirth because the vision of her newborn baby sustains her.

Even a four-year-old endures the struggle to be a very good boy for another two weeks because of a vision of gifts under a Christmas tree.

Vision is a power that motivates us to do great things, to give great things, and to love at all times. Vision keeps us going when there doesn't appear to be any other reason to keep pushing forward toward the goal.

Oswald Chambers says it is our vision of God, not our devotion to principles, nor our devotion to duty, that keeps us going for God, even when everything or everyone is tumbling and stumbling around us.

Ask God to give you a vision of who he is and how he uses you as an extension of his heart and mind.

TRUTH: TRUTH GUIDES MY STEPS

A man's steps are directed by the LORD.
How then can anyone understand his own way?
Proverbs 20:24

In faith, I know this to be true:

The Spirit of truth works within me, and he guides me to find truth wherever it can be found because all truth is God's truth (John 16:13).

The Spirit of truth encourages me to take each step of faith. He guides me to the places where I will face my fears, and as I face them in God's strength, they wither away like vines overwhelmed by the brightness of the sun.

The Spirit of truth will lead me through a wilderness meant "to uproot and tear down, to destroy and overthrow, to build and to plant" within my life (Jeremiah 1:10).

And I will fear no more, because I trust the Lord will keep me safe, and keep me true to the truth (Proverbs 29:25).

MATCHING THE FATHER'S HEART

"Love the Lord your God with all your heart."
Luke 10:27a

God wants your heart to beat in such perfect rhythm with his own that your passions merge with his passions. God wants you to love others as if your heart were one with his heart.

And the way you start loving others with a heart like God's is to first love God with all your heart. This means you focus your heart on those things that matter most to God and you let go of anything that hinders your ability to align with God's heart.

Jesus matched his heart with the Father's heart, obeying everything the Father told him to do. His heart beat so closely with the Father's that he did nothing without the Father's direction and blessing. King David was called a man after God's own heart because he cared about the things that mattered most to God and because he did what God told him to do.

Your heart can beat as one with God's. As the Holy Spirit connects you to God, his love will flow through you to others. God's plan is that your heart will eventually beat with his. He hasn't set you up for failure; he's not asking you to do something he's unwilling to support; you can match the Father's heart.

GOD IS A PARTY GOD!

Nothing in all creation is hidden from God's sight.
Everything is uncovered and laid bare before the eyes
of him to whom we must give account.
Hebrews 4:13

Miss Penelope, of Yorkie, was home alone. Her mom and dad would be home by Christmas, but for now I was the stand-in parent, asked to keep an eye on her.

One evening, as I approached Penelope's house, I heard the sound of music and entered to discover seventy-five or eighty little Yorkies all in holiday dress, dancing to "Le Freak."

Just then someone saw me and yelled, "Parent!" Every one of them scattered from the room, except Miss Penelope who just stood there and then stuck her tongue out at me!

Is it possible that we party until God shows up; and then yell, "Parent!" and scramble to where we think we can't be seen? (See Genesis 3:9.)

We forget, "Nothing in all creation is hidden from God's sight. Everything is uncovered and laid bare before the eyes of him to whom we must give account" (Hebrews 4:13).

But let's not forget that God loves a good party (John 2:1 – 11). Invite him to all your parties and he will be the life (John 4:16)!

DO YOU WANT TO BE HEALED?

When Jesus saw him lying there and learned that
he had been in this condition for a long time,
he asked him, "Do you want to get well?"
John 5:6

Long ago I was diagnosed with clinical depression. One day Jesus asked me, "Do you want to be healed?" It seemed like such a ridiculous question. Of course, I wanted to be healed!

Yet, I knew what he meant. Was I willing to do the hard work of facing painful situations, uncovering bitterness, and admitting to deep, resentful anger?

Was I willing to give up control, and admit that I can't, but he can; or would I rather insist that I can, even though I can't, holding myself in a cycle of helplessness and hopelessness?

By the pool at the Sheep Gate, Jesus asked an invalid of thirty-eight years: "Do you want to be healed?" "Sir," the invalid replied, "I have no one to help me" (John 5:7).

But there stood the Great Healer holding out help, on his way to Calvary, acutely aware that *we can't, but God can.*

The question lingers for you: *Do you really want to be healed?*

A Tree to Watch

I replied, "I see a branch of an almond tree."
The LORD said to me, "You have seen correctly,
for I watch over My word to accomplish it."
Jeremiah 1:11–12 (HCSB)

God is more faithful than the seasons we trust to come around each year. He explains this to Jeremiah in an interactive vision, where he humorously plays on the words.

In a sense, the exchange goes like this:

God of all creation: Jeremiah, what do you see?
Jeremiah: I see a branch from the "watch" tree.
God of all creation: That's right! Use it as a reminder that I "watch" over my Word, that I am constantly at work whether or not you can see what I'm doing.

In the winter a tree may appear barren; yet, there is life working within the branches that we won't see until spring.

We can trust God beyond what we see: "For in this hope we were saved. But hope that is seen is no hope at all. Who hopes for what he already has? But if we hope for what we do not yet have, we wait for it patiently" (Romans 8:24–25).

GOD IS OUR STRENGTH

God is our refuge and strength, an ever-present help in trouble.
Psalm 46:1

Bertha Smith, a storied missionary to China, once came to speak at a small Kentucky congregation where my friend Steve Pettit was pastor.

She began praying with a group of people, and when one young man said, "Lord, I just need strength; please give me strength," Bertha, a mighty prayer warrior, stopped the prayer and said, "Young man, God does not give us strength. He is our strength. Now pray it right."

In other words, he doesn't take our tattered strength and prop it up with support beams and steel cable. Instead, he moves into our weakness and there, he is strong.

May God bless Bertha, because she was more interested in teaching truth than she was in social niceties, and because she was more interested in developing disciples who know that "God can" than ones who stick to "I can, if only God will convince me that I really am strong."

Our objective-in-Jesus is to grow confident in the truth that God is our strength.

A RIGHTEOUS MESS

So Shadrach, Meshach and Abednego came out of the fire ...
and there was no smell of fire on them.
Daniel 3:26–27

One Thanksgiving I woke up in a hospital to the realization that instead of being moments away from carving the turkey, I'd been the turkey carved that day. My gallbladder was removed during emergency surgery.

Lying there, I reflected on how rough the year had been: I had a kidney stone removed, a hernia repaired, an operation on my writing hand, and my gallbladder sliced out; and we began our care of my mother diagnosed with Alzheimer's.

Yet, God taught me that being in a mess is an opportunity for him to show us how he works in our lives, and the messes we face can provoke us into more certain belief and firmer faith.

Life hurts, but truth reminds us that our life is in Christ. With the Holy Spirit empowering us, trouble becomes an opportunity to develop joy: "For you know that when your faith is tested, your endurance has a chance to grow" (James 1:3 NLT).

ABANDONING OUR FANTASIES

Godliness leads to love for other Christians, and finally
you will grow to have genuine love for everyone.
2 Peter 1:7 (NLT, 1996 ed.)

It is always easier to love philosophically or in the future tense ("Someday I will . . .") than it is to love in the reality of the present moment.

For example, it takes no effort to love the dream of your children—what they could be or should be or would be if they'd just listen to you. But, as my friend Steve Pettit says, genuinely loving the teenage child who's acting like your spouse's side of the family—that's a different matter!

In Jesus-community, we are forced from our fantasies where everyone is always accommodating and adjusting to our preferences. The standard for love isn't measured by what feels good or what we think may work; the standard for love is nothing less than the personal, loving nature of God himself.

Our objective-in-Jesus is to see, "It is no longer I who loves, but Christ who loves in me. And this difficult person I now love, I love by the faith of the Son of God, who loved him and gave himself up for him" (Galatians 2:20, author paraphrase).

An Untrustworthy God?

He is faithful in all he does ...
the earth is full of his unfailing love.
Psalm 33:4–5

God is the sovereign, supreme ruler of the universe, powerful enough to overcome any problem or defeat any enemy:

Everything comes from him;
Everything happens through him;
Everything ends up in him. (Romans 11:36 MSG)

God is always fair (Deuteronomy 32:4); he's pure and honest (Hebrews 6:18); he cannot break a promise (Numbers 23:19), never fails to fulfill a promise (Joshua 21:45), and is trustworthy in everything he does (Psalm 33:4).

God is love (1 John 4:16), and so we know he is patient and kind; he's never rude or self-seeking; he's not easily angered, and he keeps no record of wrongs; he does not delight in evil but rejoices with the truth; he always protects, always trusts, always hopes, always perseveres; he never fails (see 1 Corinthians 13:4–8).

If we doubt God, the issue is not over God's ability to support us. He clearly can do that; the issue is with our ability to trust.

I WON'T STOP LOVING YOU

A friend loves at all times, and a brother is born for adversity.
Proverbs 17:17

If your objective is to get someone to love you back, he can defeat your objective by refusing to love you. If your objective is to change someone, she can shut down your attempts to force change. If your objective is to constantly please someone, he can continue being "unpleased."

But no one can block your objective to freely give unconditional, Spirit-inspired love.

Others can reject your love, refuse your love, misunderstand your love, discount your love, spit on your love, ignore your love, or impugn your love, but no one can stop you from giving love.

They can hold your love in scorn, crown your love with thorns, and nail your love to a cross of shame, but no one can stop you from giving love.

Love presses through as "it always protects, always trusts, always hopes, always perseveres" (1 Corinthians 13:7).

The all-powerful God of love takes our fears and redeems them with his love, so that, with this unstoppable love, we are able to love others, particularly those who *appear to us* to be unlovable.

CONFIDENT IN GOD'S TRUTH

Then Caleb ... said, "We should go up and take possession
of the land, for we can certainly do it."
Numbers 13:30

Every day of your life, you have a choice: You can focus on the giants that stand before you, or you can focus on God who is pouring his strength into you.

When the Israelites approached Canaan, Moses sent scouts into the Promised Land to assess the situation. Ten of the scouts came back with reports that focused on the giants in the land whom they feared could not be defeated.

However, two of the scouts remained focused on God's promise that he would hand the land over to the Israelites. One of those scouts, Caleb, sought to silence the others when he said, "We should go up and take possession of the land, for we can certainly do it" (Numbers 13:30).

What giants are you facing that challenge your faith? God wants you to develop confidence in the truth that he's pouring his strength into you so you can do whatever it takes to defeat the giants and take possession of his abundant life.

BLIND TRUTH: EXPECTATIONS

"Go," he told him, "wash in the Pool of Siloam."
John 9:7

The blind man was desperate to be healed. He was desperate for change and desperate for a sign from God—desperate to know he hadn't been forgotten.

The blind beggar may have turned toward the voice, expecting the one speaking to command his eyes to open, expecting this man to speak light where there had only been darkness his whole life.

But Jesus didn't give the command. The blind man may not have even been aware of what Jesus was doing in that moment, working his saliva into the mud and then spreading it across the man's eyes like a mask.

Only then did Jesus give a command: "Go," he told him, "wash in the Pool of Siloam" (John 9:7).

Jesus violates expectations. He is not subject to our expectations of him; we are subject to his expectations of us. Jesus may appear inconsistent. For instance, one time he may heal someone with a mere word, but another time he may put mud in your eye! However, he is consistent with the will of the Father, matching God step-by-step.

EVERYTHING IN COMMON

All the believers were together and had everything in common.
Acts 2:44

Even before history began God lived in Trinitarian community. When he created us in his own image, he designed us with a desire to live in community.

In Christ-community we move toward oneness with God by learning to be one with each other. We are Jesus-lives, grafted and connected into the created body of Christ, with Jesus as the uncreated head.

In this Christ-body we are connected together by the same Holy Spirit working within each one of us, enabling us to unite with the one true God (cf. John 17:20–23), and giving us the same compelling force of God's inexhaustible, energizing love.

In committed community we are stretched as others can lovingly confront us about the blind spots that block us from developing wholly into healthy Jesus-ones. As iron sharpens iron, we are able to sharpen each other (Proverbs 27:17).

In Christ-community we can become who God intends us to be when we grow into a healthy, ripe-on-the-vine Jesus-one.

GET A LIFE!

"And do you seek great things for yourself?
Do not seek them; for behold, I will bring adversity
on all flesh," says the LORD. "But I will give your life to you
as a prize in all places, wherever you go."
Jeremiah 45:5 (NKJV)

We become real, healed, full human beings when we connect with Jesus through the Holy Spirit. Until then, we are still sending postcards from a fantasy life.

Our maturity in Jesus brings us closer and closer to real life — life as it was established by God before he set the foundations of the world.

Thomas Merton, the prayer-centered monk, spoke in terms of life being like an onion. God keeps peeling away the layers until the real you is revealed.

God uses adversity in your life to scrape away the layers that cover your real life. When adversity comes, there will be no time to pack a bag filled with ego, self-centeredness, lust, or materialism. God will let you escape, but only with the Jesus-clothes on your back.

What you are left with is your real life in Jesus (Colossians 3:4), where we enter into the abundance of life promised by Jesus (John 10:10).

A Worthwhile Sacrifice

We put no stumbling block in anyone's path,
so that our ministry will not be discredited.
2 Corinthians 6:3

If you are serious about serving others, you need to become seriously acquainted with sacrifice.

This comes from the apostle Paul, a man who was in and out of prison and repeatedly faced death. He labored, toiled, and went without sleep and often without any food. Paul lived exposed to the elements, sometimes not even having adequate clothing.

You may have heard it said that we want to be saints, but we don't want to live the life of a saint. We want the anointing of a powerful testimony for Jesus but at our convenience, instead of under the sovereignty of our King, who modeled sacrificial service when he "did not consider equality with God something to be grasped, but made himself nothing, taking the very nature of a servant, being made in human likeness" (Philippians 2:6–7).

Anything given to enrich the lives of others on behalf of Christ is a worthwhile sacrifice (Philippians 3:7).

GET YOUR HEAD IN THE GAME

*Forgetting what is behind and straining toward what is ahead,
I press on toward the goal to win the prize for which God
has called me heavenward in Christ Jesus.*
Philippians 3:13–14

When teams work together they become more than just a group of individuals; they move in unity with one heart and one mind—a model of oneness with God.

Teams build on the strength of each player and they adjust so that individual weaknesses become irrelevant. A unified team understands that what affects one team member also affects every team member.

On God's team, when one teammate stumbles, other team members step into the gap, physically and spiritually; when one teammate's faith falters, other teammates stand firm in their faith, confident and encouraging that God will guide and provide. They build each other up, carry each other's burdens, and celebrate one another's successes—whether large or small, collective or individual.

God didn't give us gifts just to sit and watch from the sidelines. You are part of the team. Get into the game and see God stretch you "heavenward in Christ Jesus" (Philippians 3:14).

GOTTA SERVE SOMEBODY

"For I myself am a man under authority,
with soldiers under me."
Matthew 8:9

The centurion's faith reveals the foundation of biblical humility. Instead of emphasizing his high rank, the soldier first established his place under authority. And that's really all humility is: recognizing, confessing, and acting according to your position under authority.

Because he was a man under authority, faithful to execute the orders of those in authority over him, the centurion had an expectation that those under his authority would do the same.

The centurion recognized Jesus as a man under the authority of God; he believed when Jesus gave a command, it would be obeyed because it was given under the authority of God.

Humility means we hold an accurate and unbiased assessment of who we are and whose we are, and where we belong in God's purposes and plans.

By obeying God's commands, you acknowledge your position under him—you become a man or woman under authority. And this should keep you humble when God places you in authority because the authority you have comes from your submission to him.

GRACE — NO MATTER HOW SMALL IT IS

I consider my life worth nothing to me, if only I may finish the race and complete the task the Lord Jesus has given me — the task of testifying to the gospel of God's grace.
Acts 20:24

God will use you despite your weaknesses. As God pours his grace into your life, even your weaknesses will reflect his strength.

God didn't withhold his love of you until you cleaned up your life, and he doesn't expect perfection from you before you start serving him.

He wants you — beautiful, flawed you — to show others that he is a God of redemption, a God of second chances who cares about others with weaknesses, flaws, and horrible mistakes, and a God who wants to bring them into his family.

Trust God and not your own perspective. What you see as a flaw or an irrevocable mistake may be the very thing God uses to lead people to Jesus. Your job is to be obedient to God's guidance as he directs you in mission and ministry.

No Longer Afraid

The glory of the Lord shone around them, and they were terrified. But the angel said to them, "Do not be afraid. I bring you good news of great joy that will be for all the people."
Luke 2:9 – 10

Have you ever noticed God is always telling us to not be afraid?

There are all kinds of reasons we might be afraid to receive a message from God: We are afraid of change, afraid of losing control, afraid of sacrifice. Or, perhaps, we are afraid of living apart from the mythology that we must be good enough for God.

Yet, the good news of great joy is that you don't have to be good enough: Jesus is good enough on your behalf!

As you abandon your fears, ask God to guide you toward a great faith, where you chase *him* instead of chasing perfection. God doesn't love you because you are the best in your class or because you try really hard. *God's love needs no because*; he unconditionally loves you — period.

HEDGE OF PROTECTION

For this reason I will fence her in with thornbushes.
I will block her path with a wall to make her lose her way.
Hosea 2:6 (NLT)

When Gomer, the prophet Hosea's wife, continued to chase after other lovers, God placed a hedge of protection around her, keeping her from finding adulterous relationships and eventually driving her back to her husband.

In the case of a wayward loved one, we can pray a "hedge of thorns" around someone. For instance, we can ask God to place a hedge of thorns around our children, protecting them from friends who influence them in the wrong way

On rare occasions, we may petition God to remove the hedge from our loved ones in the hope that, once they are sitting in the pig trough sharing a meal with the prodigal, they'll come to their senses and return to God (see Romans 1:18–32).

Your objective-in-Jesus is to continually pray a positive prayer of protection around you and your family, asking God to maintain a hedge that protects your loved ones from the satanic influences of the world.

HOLY ONE OF BLESSING

For from him and through him and to him are all things.
To him be the glory forever! Amen.
Romans 11:36

Lawrence Kushner, in *The Book of Words*, describes a prayer liturgy that helps us stay focused on the God who continually blesses us: "O Holy One of Blessing, your presence fills creation. Thank you _____." We are supposed to fill in the blank. For instance:

"O Holy One of Blessing, your presence fills creation. Thank you for this beautiful day."

"O Holy One of Blessing, your presence fills creation. Thank you for this music that brings me closer to you."

"O Holy One of Blessing, your presence fills creation. Thank you for this breath I take."

The prayer is a reminder of the sovereignty and majesty of God. In that truth, the prayer can even be used when it appears that nothing good—no blessing—can come from a situation, such as a disfiguring car accident or the death of a child in the womb. We can acknowledge God's blessings, even when we have no real desire to do so: "O Holy One of Blessing, your presence fills creation. It is up to you to judge these circumstances."

IGNITING THE ENGINE-OF-US

For we are ... created in Christ Jesus to do good works,
which God prepared in advance for us to do.
Ephesians 2:10

Our oneness with God enables us to do good works. Any work done without the enabling power of God, despite our good intentions, is an act without faith. It is a *faith-less* act.

Walk with me on this:

The French mathematician and theological journalist Blasé Pascal suggests we were created with a God-shaped hole within us that only Jesus can fill. This God-shaped hole remains empty until we give up our rebellion against God and allow him to fill us with his Spirit.

When God's Spirit fills the God-shaped hole, we become fully human. Ian Thomas explains that next, when the fuel of the Holy Spirit ignites within the engine-of-us, we begin to do the good works God planned for us.

By faith, we move and live and have our being in Christ through this Holy Spirit ignition within us. Our good works come through this connection—not from the things we do apart from our connection with God, no matter how well-intentioned they are.

JESUS WEPT

Jesus wept.
John 11:35

Jesus wept. Jesus was deeply aware of the suffering around him, and he wanted to relieve it. Jesus is also very aware of your hurts and fears, and he wants to relieve them.

Being sensitively aware of how others are suffering is the core of compassion. It's more than a heartfelt acknowledgment that someone else is in hardship or pain; it enters into the sorrow and the pain of others, working to relieve those who suffer.

Being compassionate is part of God's nature, and is a characteristic of Jesus. The more we become like Jesus, the more compassion will become a part of our character.

Compassion re-creates us as a safe place to which others can bring their failures and frustrations, knowing that instead of being judged they will be loved by someone who resembles the face of Jesus.

Compassion sets us on a history-making journey to do the work of God right here, right now as we become beacons of God's compassion in a world full of people who are isolated, ignored, and abandoned.

Jesus wept. Jesus-ones weep too.

LIES OF OMISSION

*We will not be influenced when people try to trick us
with lies so clever they sound like the truth.*
Ephesians 4:14 (NLT, 1996 ed.)

My brother got caught in a lie once while sitting at a stoplight. He told my parents he was heading down to Allen's Drive-in, not unusual because it was just a few miles from our house. What he didn't tell them is he was actually driving sixty miles away to an Allen's in Kansas City, Missouri.

My brother didn't count on Mom and Dad heading over to Kansas City to do some Christmas shopping. There sat my brother waiting for the light to turn green when up pulled my parents in the lane next to him.

My brother told a lie of omission (and I'm using his example and not many of my own). He told the truth, but not the whole truth, deceiving by leaving out critical information and, thereby, leaving a false impression.

Many of us would never consider telling an outright lie. Yet, we habitually tell lies of omission to make ourselves look better or to simply get our own way.

Our objective-in-Jesus is to speak the whole truth and nothing but the truth, so help us God, as we grow toward the full maturity of Christ (Ephesians 4:13).

LIVING ANTI-FAITH

For I am convinced that neither death nor life,
neither angels nor demons, neither the present nor the future,
nor any powers, neither height nor depth, nor anything else
in all creation, will be able to separate us from the love
of God that is in Christ Jesus our Lord.
Romans 8:38–39

When we fear making mistakes, we become timid and limit ourselves from living life abundantly. We let paralysis hinder our decisions as we lead quiet, desperate, anti-faith lives, afraid to move with the bold confidence God's grace gives us to walk in times of uncertainty (Hebrews 10:19–25).

Martin Luther, fighting against this insipid timidity, wrote, "Be a sinner, and let your sins be strong, but let your trust in Christ be stronger, and rejoice in Christ who is the victor over sin, death, and the world."

Luther isn't excusing sin; he's restoring God's grace to its proper position. We can live boldly, no longer in fear of making mistakes, because "we are more than conquerors through him who loved us" (Romans 8:37).

NOWHERE ELSE TO GO

For if the willingness is there, the gift is acceptable according to what one has, not according to what he does not have.
2 Corinthians 8:12

Often, God asks us to make the choice to do his will before we know the specific details of his plan. That's because part of God's plan is to develop in us a trust of his character and his benevolence.

He wants us to trust him with complete abandonment, believing that his will is the best plan, believing that he will strengthen us to do all that he asks.

One reason God doesn't give us the full picture of his plans is that we may be overwhelmed by what we see; it may appear impossible to us.

God will not be surprised by your transparency if you say, "Father, I'm not sure I'm ready to do your will. I don't know if I want to do it or not."

Allow God to strengthen you in this area. Tell him, "I don't know that I'm willing to step out in faith without first knowing everything that's going to happen, but I'm willing to be made willing."

DID YOU LOSE
ANYTHING OF VALUE?

"How much more valuable is a man than a sheep!"
Matthew 12:12

The intruder was in her den when she walked in. She didn't see him at first, but she could sense something wasn't right.

And then he ran to attack her. Struggling on the floor, she reached for anything to defend herself and grabbed some scissors she had in a basket full of coupons.

Fearing for her life, she swung the scissors down as hard as she possibly could and killed the man.

And I thought, "Wow, this is a pretty intense episode."

I have told you about this, though, because of what the homeowner said when the police arrived. To identify what the intruder was after one of them asked the woman, "Do you have anything of value in your house?"

What would your response be? Some jewelry? A widescreen TV? A cutting-edge computer? An irreplaceable family heirloom?

You know what she said when asked if there was anything of value in her house?

"Yes, my nine-year-old daughter."

How much more valuable are your relationships than things!

NON-SELECTIVE COMPASSION

*"I tell you the truth, whatever you did for one of the least
of these brothers of mine, you did for me."*
Matthew 25:40

We are like Jesus when we serve others. After washing his disciples' feet, Jesus said, "I have given you an example to follow. Do as I have done to you" (John 13:15 NLT).

The compassion of Jesus is not selective. He teaches us to help those in need regardless of how we feel about them or what we think about them.

Jesus said: "For I was hungry, and you fed me. I was thirsty, and you gave me a drink. I was a stranger, and you invited me into your home. I was naked, and you gave me clothing. I was sick, and you cared for me. I was in prison, and you visited me" (Matthew 25:35 – 36 NLT).

This kind of compassion concentrates so intently on others that we forget ourselves in the moment. Like Jesus, we empty ourselves, taking on the form of a servant (Philippians 2:7). In serving the "least of these," we show others what Jesus-in-action looks like and, at the same time, we show Jesus that we love him.

RISKY OBEDIENCE

Risk your life and get more than you ever dreamed of.
Luke 19:26 (MSG)

Risk means we are compelled to action, even when there seems to be no guarantee of what will be on the other side of our choice of faith.

If we believe what we say we believe, regardless of what we see on the other side of faithful risk, the reality is God is there. What seems to be a no-guarantee situation actually comes with a *God-guarantee* — that he is working it all out (Jeremiah 29:11; Romans 8:28). With a God-guarantee:

- You can attempt things that are impossible unless God gives you his strength to do them.
- You can love other believers so deeply that you prove to the world you bear God's fathomless love.
- You can change your priorities to match God's priorities.
- You can go make disciples of all peoples, "baptizing them in the name of the Father and of the Son and of the Holy Spirit" (Matthew 28:19).

SPEAKING GOD'S NATIVE TONGUE

*"When he lies, he speaks his native language,
for he is a liar and the father of lies."*
John 8:44

We are fluent in the native language of the Devil; we lie to others, we lie to ourselves, we lie to God.

Satan is the "father of lies" (John 8:44), giving birth to black lies, white lies, little fibs, and outrageous whoppers, even those "misspoken" or "misunderstood."

Yet, God would have us speak in his native tongue, the romance language of love. It's a language so different from the Devil's tongue that it is unintelligible to those fluent in his deception dialect (John 8:43, 47).

"We don't twist God's Word to suit ourselves. Rather, we keep everything we do and say out in the open, the whole truth on display, so that those who want to can see and judge for themselves in the presence of God" (2 Corinthians 4:2 MSG).

The Father's language of love speaks without lies. As new creations in Christ, our objective-in-Jesus is to no longer speak in the Devil's tongue (Colossians 3:9), and by doing this we become consistent with God's character, not the Devil's (John 8:44 NLT).

THE OBEDIENCE OF GRAVITY

"I am the Lord's servant," Mary answered.
"May it be to me as you have said."
Luke 1:38

When God sent an angel to Mary to tell her that even as a virgin she would conceive the child Jesus, she responded with immediate obedience.

Our objective-in-Jesus is for obedience to become so natural that we do it without even thinking. You can think of it this way: Gravity is so faithful to do what God designed it to do that we can't even imagine gravity being disobedient to God or inconsistent to its nature.

As impossible as it may sound, we are to become so obedient to God that those who know us cannot imagine us ever doing anything inconsistent with the life of Christ, who works within us.

In that moment, we become so much the person God designed us to be that, in paradox, denying self and serving others seems a natural part of our character.

THERE IS A RIVER

Such a one is like a tree planted near streams;
it bears fruit in season and its leaves never wither,
and every project succeeds.
Psalm 1:3 (NJB)

There is a river that flows from the throne of God and down the celestial main street, and those who believe in the Lamb receive nourishment from that water (Revelation 22; Psalm 1:3); the river then flows like streams of living water through those who are united with Jesus (John 7).

We hear the river whisper, "If anyone is thirsty, let him come to me and drink" (John 7:37). We feel its moisture hanging cool in the air, and we stretch and then we stretch again to reach the river's edge.

It woos us to dwell within it, to dig deep with determined roots, gnarled fingers inching, bit by bit, toward the source of life.

Rooted at the river, we stand firm against the storms and we sip sweetly in times of drought, even as others burn up or blow away when faced with the dry and dusty times of life.

Nourished by the river of life, the fruit we produce is "love, joy, peace, patience, kindness, goodness, faithfulness, gentleness and self-control" (Galatians 5:22–23).

WE IS STRONGER THAN ME

I planted the seed, Apollos watered it, but God made it grow ... The man who plants and the man who waters have one purpose, and each will be rewarded according to his own labor.
1 Corinthians 3:6, 8

We can draw strength and encouragement from each other as we bring people into God's presence. We don't have to do it alone; God intends for us to work together—as "we," not just "me."

Evangelism is always a team effort, even in those times when we think we are working alone. When we lead someone to Christ, the Holy Spirit has already been at work in that person's life, and other believers have also been influential, directly and indirectly.

Pray with some other Jesus-ones: "Father, develop in us a deep concern for those who are not yet one with Jesus, and prompt us to pray consistently for their salvation. Give us an inventive creativity and a contagious enthusiasm as we tell others about your love and forgiveness. We lift this prayer in the name of your precious Son, Jesus. Amen."

WHEN YOU TURN BACK
FROM TURNING BACK

"But I have prayed for you, Simon, that your faith may not fail. And when you have turned back, strengthen your brothers."
Luke 22:32

Jesus told Peter: "Satan has asked to sift you as wheat" (Luke 22:31).

A sifting probes your weaknesses, revealing the distractions that hinder you from fulfilling your purpose. In Peter's case, the sifting scraped away Peter's stomp, snort, and bluster, re-creating in him a teachable heart.

Consider the grace note Jesus uses to tell Peter about the sifting. He didn't just say, "Get ready for a whirlwind of hurt! I know you're going to let me down."

Instead, Jesus pointed to the future: Peter would survive the sifting; he would return humbled, but stronger, with the purpose to strengthen his brothers.

In a sense, Jesus says, "When you turn back from your turning back, you'll be a servant who leads."

You may have days when you wonder if God is letting Satan sift you. Your objective-in-Jesus is to develop a radiant certainty that no matter what, God is in control and that he who is in you is greater than he who is in the world (1 John 4:4).

YOU "MERCIED" ME

*Therefore, since through God's mercy we have
this ministry, we do not lose heart.*
2 Corinthians 4:1

My youngest son sometimes gets creative with his use of words. My favorite example is when he said, "Dad, you nervoused me!" meaning, "You made me nervous!"

I use this illustration to help you remember Paul's words in 2 Corinthians 4:1, where he says in effect, "We have been 'mercied' by God."

The flood of God's mercy sweeps us toward an intimate relationship with him, the strong current pushing us into oneness with our gracious and *merciful* Creator.

And so Paul says, because of God's great mercy, we now have this ministry of reconciliation. Through God's mercy we are energized to tell others about God's mercy. The good news we carry is that the very Spirit of the living God now works in us and through us.

You need not lose heart, says Paul, because you have been "mercied" by God, and he is transforming your heart with hope.

CONFESSION AND JETTISON

Who may ascend the hill of the LORD?
Who may stand in his holy place?
Psalm 24:3

Preparing our hearts for worship requires we cleanse ourselves of anything that comes between us and God.

The psalmist declares that someone who can stand on God's holy hill "has clean hands and a pure heart ... does not lift up his soul to an idol or swear by what is false" (Psalm 24:4).

The Holy Spirit's work is to make us aware of where our hands are not clean and our hearts are not pure. Then, our job is to confess those sins and jettison them from our lives—confession and jettison.

"Father, before you I stand. Cleanse me from top to bottom; root out the sin strongholds in my mind and bring me to a place where I am walking purely and where my prayers are more for others than for my self-centered self.

"Guide me in your way everlasting as I walk in the knowledge of the holiness you've freely given me: I cannot work my way into holiness, but you give it to me through Jesus Christ, my Lord."

REPRESENTATIVE LIES

*Do not lie to each other, since you have taken off your old self
with its practices and have put on the new self, which is being
renewed in knowledge in the image of its Creator.*
Colossians 3:9–10

When we think of lies, we usually think about lies of commission, where we specifically make false statements.

Most of us would never think of telling a blatant lie. But, we often live with a lie of commission so subtle it is easy to dismiss it without much of a thought. Such a lie is often exaggeration: an unbalanced, unfair representation of how things happened or our pejorative interpretation of what actually happened

It's when we say, "Nobody would help me," when, in truth, we only asked one person. It's when we say, "Everybody hated it," when, in truth, two people out of two hundred disliked it.

We denigrate others in order to maintain the lie that we are not in any way responsible for a conflict or misunderstanding.

Instead of facing the truth about ourselves, prompting us to pluck the plank out of our own eye, we recast the other person to make their sawdust look like a lumber yard.

And that is living a lie.

COVER ME

*Above all, love each other deeply, because love
covers over a multitude of sins.*
1 Peter 4:8

One of the classic bonding moments in movies is when
two characters are not getting along, but one is about to get in
trouble. The other character covers for the person and helps
him or her past a momentary lapse in judgment or a foolish
mistake. In that moment they bond as friends, knowing they
can trust each other no matter what.

In the same sense, we are to cover for our brothers and
sisters, deeply loving them into their best. When a brother
or sister falters, when a family member fails, when we trip
up and hurt ourselves and others, we can run to one another
for cover.

When sin sneaks in, we keep one another from greater
corruption. When wounded, we protect one another from
greater injury.

Our objective-in-Jesus is to begin providing cover for our
brothers and sisters; to make a choice to see them for what
they are becoming—not for what they once were, or even
what they may now be.

SAME OLD, SAME OLD

*The shepherds returned, glorifying and praising God
for all the things they had heard and seen.*
Luke 2:20

After we celebrate the birth of Jesus, we return to the office, we return to school, we return to the things we normally do.

The shepherds of Bethlehem did the same thing. God sent them to find the baby Jesus in a manger. They marveled at God and knew they had been blessed to see the Messiah's arrival. Later, they returned to their fields and flocks, glorifying and praising God. But they still returned to their routine.

God takes us to the mountaintop where he shows us great miracles and wonders, but he doesn't leave us there. It's in the fields and among the flocks that our faith grows, nurtured in the soil of day-to-day mundaneness. This is where we die to Christ, allowing his life to blossom within us (Galatians 2:20).

It's conflicts over who makes the coffee, who cleans up the mess, who gets to go home early, or who gets the biggest piece of pie that test whether it is Christ who lives in us or whether we are still saying, "It is I who live."

DO YOUR BEST TO REST

Therefore, since the promise of entering his rest
still stands, let us be careful that none of you be found
to have fallen short of it.
Hebrews 4:1

Most of us think of the Sabbath as a day of rest, but it carries a larger significance. It is an invitation to rest in God's healing grace, trusting in his power and purpose for your life.

Ian Thomas illustrates this point by telling the story of a man walking down a dusty, rural road loaded down with a heavy backpack and carrying a duffle bag in each hand. A pickup truck comes along, and the driver lets the man hop in the back.

The driver heads down the road, but when he looks in the rearview mirror, he sees his passenger is standing in the bed of the truck still holding both duffle bags, still wearing the over-packed backpack on his back.

We stand in the truck of faith, still carrying our burdens. But God's truck of faith is big enough to carry us and all our burdens. Sit down and rest in the ride of God that is carrying us home to him.

TRUTH: GOD WANTS ME TO SUCCEED

Now to him who is able to do immeasurably more than all we ask or imagine, according to his power that is at work within us.
Ephesians 3:20

In faith, I know this to be true: God wants me to succeed in my walk of faith.

His power works within me to do immeasurably more than I can ever ask or imagine. He planned that I succeed at my purpose, created me to succeed at my purpose, and is now going before and coming behind me as I fulfill my purpose (Ephesians 2:10; Psalm 139:5).

In my frustration, I may see his plans as evil, but they are actually plans full of "hope and a future" (Jeremiah 29:11). He is not a thief who has come to "steal and kill and destroy"; he has come to give me life, a life full and complete and with purpose (John 10:10).

God enlightens the eyes of my heart so that I can see the hope to which he has called me, "the riches of his glorious inheritance in the saints" (Ephesians 1:18). My objective-in-Jesus is to grow confident in the truth that God is clearing the path for my success.

OBJECTIVE-IN-JESUS: A VOICE

John replied in the words of Isaiah the prophet,
"I am the voice of one calling in the desert,
'Make straight the way for the Lord.'"
John 1:23

Like Isaiah and John the Baptist, you are the "voice of one calling in the desert, 'Make straight the way for the Lord'" (John 1:23).

Because you speak as a Jesus-one, your objective is to reach the place where you can say: "The message I bring is from God; it's not anything I thought of on my own. The words I speak are not the result of human wisdom or human imagination or my own opinion; they were formed in me by the Holy Spirit so that I could express 'spiritual truths in spiritual words' (1 Corinthians 2:12–13)."

In order for God's message to grow in me and to grow in you, "he must increase" and "I must decrease" (John 3:30 NKJV).

The more I live the message, the more God increases in me; the more I decrease, the more God's message flowing through me comes to you pure—unfiltered and uncontaminated by my opinions, prejudices, demands, and self-reliance.

I'm not the message; I'm the messenger. I'm a God-created, God-cleansed, God-commanded voice.

WHEN FEAR WALKS IN

Because the one who is in you is greater
than the one who is in the world.
1 John 4:4

When fear enters a room, I fear you and your intention. I fear for myself and what you may cost me. I stay on my side and refuse to move toward you.

When fear reigns, I can't reveal who I am. I'm so concerned about protecting my goods that I'm afraid to give anything to you.

When God walks in, I lay down my fears and give up my self-absorption. Jesus offers an uncommon safety to be me—to be real, to be sad, to be messed up and confused, yet, to be loved. And as that safety saturates the room, I can offer it to you because my faith in God is stronger than my faith in fear.

The world accommodates fear because it does not know God, but we are children of God, drenched in our Father's love (1 John 3:1–2). When fear knocks at the door, we fall on the faith that "the one who is in you is greater than the one who is in the world" (1 John 4:4).

SOMEBODY'S TO BLAME

"Shall we accept good from God, and not trouble?"
Job 2:10

It was a frustrating situation and I was looking for someone to blame: "Maybe it was his fault, maybe it was her fault, maybe it was their fault." I even thought, finally, "Maybe it's my fault," so I kicked myself emotionally for a few days.

In one of my clearer moments, I told a friend, "I really want to find someone to blame in this situation, but there's just no one to blame. It's just one of those things that happen."

Life is hard, but Jesus lives. Accept that the sun shines on both those who chase after God and those who defiantly run from him. Job, as he scraped the sores on his skin, having lost virtually everything, said, "Shall we accept good from God, and not trouble?" (Job 2:10).

Rush to God, not to blame. Instead of blaming someone for your situation, take your frustrations to God. The poet, King David, constantly cried out to God, honestly, sometimes angrily, singing his psalms with a courageous authenticity. David's conversation with God drew him closer to God, transforming David into a man after God's own heart.

Spiritual Pacifism

This is no afternoon athletic contest that we'll
walk away from and forget about in a couple of hours.
This is for keeps, a life-or-death fight to the finish
against the Devil and all his angels.
Ephesians 6:12 (MSG)

God wants us strong, so he has placed weapons of righteousness at our disposal. These weapons require us to work with him, relying on him when we come up against the enemy.

Our objective-in-Jesus is to learn to utilize weapons of the Spirit, such as honesty, humility, authenticity, grace, love, prayer, obedience, community, healthy dependence, God's Word, and the Holy Spirit's guidance. In contrast, weapons of the flesh include such things as excessive anger, manipulation, blame, shame, hatred, pride, sneaky hiding, self-centeredness, defensiveness, and an unhealthy "I don't need you" attitude.

The spiritual battle that we are engaged in is a cataclysmic, brutal, and bloody war of eternal significance. Yet, in this war we have God with us, God in us, and God for us.

How long will we be inactive and neutral Christians in this cosmic war?

BLOCKING ACCESS TO HEAVEN

*"You shut the kingdom of heaven in men's faces. You yourselves
do not enter, nor will you let those enter who are trying to."*
Matthew 23:13

Imagine you are heading into a hotel with an invitation from the owner. But when you get there, you find an official-looking group of men blocking the entrance to the hotel.

They say you have to meet a dozen or so regulations before you can enter. The list they hand you is a painstakingly technical set of requirements that distracts you from your appointment with the owner.

Suddenly, the owner appears, genuinely concerned about your whereabouts. He looks at the list in your hand and looks at the men who gave you the list, and says:

"You hypocrites! You've blocked the door to my hotel! You've made it so you can't get in and neither can anyone else.

"If you're concerned about requirements, let me sum them up for you: Love God, love your neighbor, love yourself, and admit that you gain entrance to the hotel through my loving generosity and not your miserly methods."

And this is why Jesus felt such grief for the Pharisees.

TRANSFIGURATION AND TRANSFORMATION

"Rabbi, it is good for us to be here. Let us put up three shelters—one for you, one for Moses and one for Elijah."
Mark 9:5

When Jesus took Peter, James, and John to the Mount of Transfiguration, he transformed right before their eyes (Mark 9:2–3). Then, without warning, Elijah and Moses appeared with Jesus.

Peter responded as we too often respond. He wanted to build a monument to commemorate the greatness of the place and the significance of the moment. But God spoke up and in a sense said: "Look, skip the monuments. Skip the building. Here's what I want you to do: Listen to my Son, whom I love. Listen to him!" (based on Mark 9:7).

Moreover, Jesus could have gone on to say, "Peter, I am in charge of building the monuments—and you are one of them. You and James and John and anyone who believes in me become a monument of my grace. Just as my appearance changed from the inside out, I am doing the same to you—pressing the pure, white light of forgiveness and grace through you, so others can see it and know that I am God."

THE MYTHOLOGY OF FORGIVENESS

"And when you stand praying, if you hold anything against anyone, forgive him, so that your Father in heaven may forgive you your sins."
Mark 11:25

When we insist someone must meet certain conditions before we will forgive them, we enter in a mythology, where forgiveness is earned instead of freely given. It's a mythology contrary to God.

Three forgiveness myths are noted by Rick Warren in his book *The Purpose Driven Life*:

"I'll forgive when he proves he should be forgiven." Biblical forgiveness doesn't carry any conditions. God gives you forgiveness freely because Jesus paid the bloody price of your debt of sin on the cross.

"If I forgive, she will get away with what she did." When you forgive, you are not letting her get away with what she did. She will still face the consequences of her behavior.

"If I forgive him, he will keep hurting me." Forgiveness doesn't mean your relationship remains the same. You may need time to trust again. If his offense is abusive or places you in danger, you can forgive him, but maintain your distance.

Our objective-in-Jesus is to develop the ability to forgive unconditionally.

FELLOWSHIP REQUIRES FAITH

*"Give to the one who asks you, and do not turn away
from the one who wants to borrow from you."*
Matthew 5:42

When we think of fellowship, we think in terms of belonging. We belong to our congregations, to a group of friends, to our families, and to each other.

God stitched the thread of belonging into the human fabric, and no doubt many of the problems we face in the nasty-now-and-now are because our longing to belong, in some way, goes unfulfilled.

It takes faith to belong: faith to face the fear of rejection; faith to experience real rejection; faith to commit to others; and faith to stay committed when others prove to be the very people you feared you would find.

When we "submit to one another out of reverence for Christ," we do it or don't do it based on our faith that God will work within the situation (Ephesians 5:21). Our reluctance to submit is because we are uncertain God will take care of our needs, particularly if we submit to someone we are quite certain will not meet our needs

Our objective-in-Jesus is to enter fellowship knowing that transparent, authentic, intimate relationships require faith in the God who created us for fellowship.

SCORING POINTS WITH GOD

But now God has shown us a way to be made right with him
without keeping the requirements of the law, as was promised
in the writings of Moses and the prophets long ago.
Romans 3:21

Brett Favre has established several significant NFL records. He set the record for most touchdown passes by a quarterback (421), and he tied another record, most interceptions thrown by an NFL quarterback (277).

We tend to think of life as a balance sheet that we will eventually present to God. As long as the number of our touchdown passes exceeds the number of our interceptions, we are cool with God, right?

It doesn't matter how many touchdowns you score; it doesn't matter how many interceptions you throw. God loves you and wants you on his team.

There is no way you could ever meet God's standard, but the good news is you don't have to because Jesus covers your sins, allowing you to become intimate with God. This freedom, in Christ, means you can be who you were meant to be and live how you were meant to live. Love God and live accordingly!

Are You Confident That God Delivers?

"The LORD is my rock, my fortress and my deliverer."
2 Samuel 22:2

Do you sometimes find yourself asking, "God, is there any kind of plan here?" or, "God, do you realize what's about to happen — *to me*?"

Each time we face a "God, what's the plan here?" moment, we have the opportunity to grow stronger in our certainty that even when things look bad, God is working it all out for our good (Jeremiah 29:11; Romans 8:28).

We have the opportunity to travel to the place where we no longer need to know how we will be delivered because we know, no matter what, "God is our Deliverer."

Our objective-in-Jesus is to seek God's face, not what is in God's hand; we chase after the Giver, not what he gives. As we move into an intimate relationship with our Creator, our confidence that he, our Deliverer, will truly deliver, grows.

If you could believe with absolute confidence that God will come through, how would your life change? What's stopping you from developing that confidence?

PATIENCE WITH IMPERFECTION

A man's wisdom gives him patience;
it is to his glory to overlook an offense.
Proverbs 19:11

Humorist Dave Barry says, "A perfect parent is a person with excellent child-rearing theories and no actual children." The same could be said of a perfect world: there's only one way to mess things up — people! Living with imperfect people requires patience, and you, like me, are one of the imperfect people who require patience.

Patience means putting up with me when you'd rather lose your temper. It means forgiving me when you'd rather nurture a grudge. Patience muzzles a mouth full of murmurs and then passes them along as prayer requests. Patience puts the *long* in long-suffering.

Patience and a critical spirit are mutually exclusive. Even when your complaints are justified, patience leads you to forgive and forget: "A man's wisdom gives him patience; it is to his glory to overlook an offense" (Proverbs 19:11).

Being patient may try our patience, but we become stronger when we learn to love imperfect people.

THE WITCHCRAFT OF REBELLION

For rebellion is as the sin of witchcraft.
1 Samuel 15:23 (NKJV)

Most of us would be shocked and angered if we found out a believer in our congregation was actively using a form of witchcraft to control people, places, things, and circumstances. In spite of our fear, we would fight back once we learned the witchcraft was so powerful it had entrapped whole families and small groups of people within the church.

Unwittingly, there is a form of witchcraft employed by many believers. It is an incantation of rebellion and disobedience to God, a sin that the prophet Samuel says is equivalent to witchcraft.

The two are similar because both work independent of God to control or change circumstances. Witchcraft casts spells and summons spirits to alter a situation, and therefore assumes a role it does not have authority to hold. Rebellion uses disobedience, disharmony, and disunity to gain or maintain control of a situation.

By using them you become one with the enemy, aligned with the very things that are in armed rebellion against God.

"Not doing what GOD tells you is far worse than fooling around in the occult," says the prophet Samuel (1 Samuel 15:23 MSG).

CREATIVE GENEROSITY

God has given gifts to each of you from his great variety
of spiritual gifts. Manage them well so that God's
generosity can flow through you.
1 Peter 4:10 (NLT, 1996 ed.)

What God gives is meant to be shared. He wants us to bless others on his behalf, and so he designed each of us with a unique combination of talents, skills, gifts, and abilities. We receive from God, then give to others: "Be generous with the different things God gave you, passing them around so all get in on it" (1 Peter 4:10 MSG).

Be creative with generosity. If you are a mechanic, help single women in your church keep their cars in good condition. If you are handy with tools, do simple repairs for some of the families in your congregation or, as a witness, for families in your neighborhood. If you are known for hospitality, teach a younger generation how to open their homes to others.

The thing is, your generosity isn't *limited* to money or service at the church — your generosity can include the many blessings, gifts, and talents God has given you. Give serious, *intentional* thought to how you can use them.

THE HOLY SPIRIT WARNING

*For the Spirit teaches you everything you need to know,
and what he teaches is true.*
1 John 2:27 (NLT)

Here are three ways the Holy Spirit speaks to us:

Spirit warning: A Spirit nudge may be a warning against impending danger. Once, a friend of mine was driving toward an intersection, but sensed a strong prompting from the Spirit to hit his brakes. He did, just as a semi ran a red light. Had it not been for his instant obedience, my friend would have been killed.

Spirit stop: A Spirit nudge may be a red flag telling you not to go somewhere. A dog I owned years ago helped me understand this. When I would take him to a field to run, I would simply say "No" when he headed somewhere he should not go. My warning was not a rebuke that he'd done wrong, but a caution, spoken for his own protection, when he was headed the wrong way.

Spirit shush: If we listen, the Spirit gives similar nudges when we are in conversations. He may prompt us when we are too close to a sinful topic, an unfair comment, or gossip.

We Learn When We Observe

Follow my example, as I follow the example of Christ.
1 Corinthians 11:1

Black smoke rose in a shaky image taken from a helicopter hovering over a neighborhood in Miami, Florida, known as Liberty City. At street level, a riot raged with eighteen people dead and 850 arrested.

My dad sat with me watching the violence on television. In a matter-of-fact manner, my dad, a special investigator in the Miami-Dade area, said, "That's exactly where I'm scheduled to be today." His current assignment was unrelated to the riot.

I asked, "Why go there in the middle of a riot?"

A strong but gentle man, my dad looked at me and replied, "Why wouldn't I go? It's my job to go."

This was an "Aha!" moment for me. Of course he would go. He had made a commitment. He was going to be where he was supposed to be, regardless of the circumstances or the difficulty or how unreasonable it might seem, even in the face of chaotic adversity.

My dad communicated more by what he did than by what he said. For me, his example became the story of God at work in a human life.

No Condemnation

Therefore, there is now no condemnation for those who are in Christ Jesus, because through Christ Jesus the law of the Spirit of life set me free from the law of sin and death.
Romans 8:1–2

No matter what you have ever done, there is no condemnation in Christ. He sits at the Father's right hand, not as your accuser, but as your advocate willing to give his life for you.

Like the heavenly Father, Jesus desires to give you mercy, not condemnation (Hosea 6:6). In a sense, he says: "The things you offer to do and the promises you want to make in exchange for your forgiveness—they're just offerings to help you get over your guilt. I'd rather give you forgiveness and grace as a gift; you don't have to win back my love. You never lost my love!"

"My purpose is not to condemn you but to let my life run free within you as the Holy Spirit connects you directly to the Father" (Romans 8:1–2, author paraphrase).

Jesus-one, when you feel condemnation coming at you like a furious flood, stand firm on the Rock, who said, "I no longer condemn you. Go and sin no more" (cf. John 8:11).

Could You Be Mistaken
for a Servant?

And I pray that you, being rooted and established in love,
may have power, together with all the saints, to grasp how
wide and long and high and deep is the love of Christ.
Ephesians 3:17 – 18

Jesus didn't care if someone mistook him for a servant with a towel; he always appeared to be more interested in actually serving than in attempting to impress.

Can you see how much trust Jesus had in the Father, that he would lay down all of his privileges in order to pick up the towel and bowl of a servant? When you understand who you are and whose you are, you will become comfortable taking the towel instead of the spotlight.

What we see in Jesus is what God wants in us: one who fully grasps the magnitude of God's love, allowing the length, width, depth, and height of his love to seep into our deepest parts. His love scrubs away our insecurities and gives us a fresh-scented energy, a cleansing grace that helps us serve others with the humility of Jesus.

SLOW, SINLESS ANGER

My dear brothers, take note of this: Everyone should be quick to listen, slow to speak and slow to become angry, for man's anger does not bring about the righteous life that God desires.
James 1:19–20

The slammed door, the "if looks could kill" stare, the menacing tone, the threatening language. The silence, the cold shoulder, the eyes that flash, the pointed finger, the phrase that blames.

These are all weapons of the flesh that express our lack of faith. Even when our anger is an appropriate emotion for the circumstance, we still grab instinctively for the most convenient weapon of the flesh instead of relying on God's weapons of the Spirit (2 Corinthians 10).

In using weapons of faithlessness, we reveal how little faith we have that God can, or will, engage the frustrating people and situations we face. We expose our deep, inner belief that God is incapable of hammering out appropriate justice.

Instead of seeking your anger, seek God. Your anger will not bring about God's righteousness. However, God takes care of our most basic needs—even our need for justice—as we "seek first his kingdom and his righteousness" (Matthew 6:33).

Truth: I Am Becoming Other-Centered

*And my God will meet all your needs according to
his glorious riches in Christ Jesus.*
Philippians 4:19

In faith, I know this to be true: By God's grace, I am becoming other-centered, no longer focused on my interests.

I can look out for the interests of others because I know it is true that God will supply all my needs, according to his riches. In faith, I know it is true that I can give more than people expect; I can help more than people may request. I am ready and enabled by God to give to anyone who asks (Matthew 5:40–42).

The life of Jesus in me is working to "do good, to be rich in good deeds, and to be generous and willing to share" (1 Timothy 6:18). And again and again, I will stand on the truth that God will meet all my needs. Therefore, I can keep an intentional focus on supplying the needs of others.

I am like Jesus when I look to the needs of others.

JESUS ACCEPTS YOU

Accept one another, then, just as Christ accepted you,
in order to bring praise to God.
Romans 15:7

Jesus accepts us, despite our messy lives, impure motives, and irritating attitudes (Ephesians 2:4–5). His acceptance doesn't condone any sin; rather, it recognizes we are God's workmanship, each of us shaped for a specific purpose in him (Ephesians 2:10).

Jesus was not afraid to be friends with unbelievers, looking past the sin in their lives to see who God created them to be. He understood that accepting the person is not the same thing as accepting their sins. As the old saying goes, "Love the sinner, not the sin."

When Jesus called Matthew to be a disciple (Matthew 9), some religious leaders asked why he was associating with people who they judged should be outcast. Jesus responded to their inquiry by saying, "It is not the healthy who need a doctor, but the sick" (Luke 5:31).

As a doctor accepts a patient regardless of the disease, Jesus accepts us — he loves us — in our present condition, and like a doctor, his intent is to heal us of our sin. Knowing you are accepted — *really accepted* — by Jesus, how will you live differently?

What Do You Mean, God?

"This will be a sign to you: You will find a baby
wrapped in cloths and lying in a manger." . . .
So they hurried off and found Mary and Joseph,
and the baby, who was lying in the manger.
Luke 2:12, 16

The interaction between the angel and the shepherds in Luke 2 shows a simple, yet significant sequence. The angel told them they would find a baby "lying in a manger" and when the shepherds reached Bethlehem, there was the baby, "lying in a manger." God told them what they would find, and that is exactly what they did find.

You and I would live differently if we followed a similar sequence. When God says it, we know it is true. And when we follow what we are told, we see that God's promise is true.

Choose today to faithfully respond to what you hear God telling you to do and rest in his grace, knowing he wants you to succeed.

COMPROMISING AT LOVE?

He is the head of the body, the church; he is the beginning
and the firstborn from among the dead, so that
in everything he might have the supremacy.
Colossians 1:18

If our love for one another is not energized by Jesus, we are doomed to slide, like the Beatles, from the promise of "All You Need Is Love" into the push and shove of "I, Me, Mine." Our love for one another cannot stop at "let's just get along" because deep and ancient God-love emerges — not from compromise, but from sacrifice.

And the first step of sacrifice is submission — not submission to one another, although that will often be required — but an uncompromising submission to Jesus, our Lord, our brother, and our King.

Jesus is the "head of the body" (Colossians 1:18). Submit to the head of our body, and he will show you how to love others with a deep Jesus-love. It is his power and his strength that will energize you to love even those you find impossible to love.

GUT-WRENCHING COMPASSION

When he saw the crowds, he had compassion on them, because they were harassed and helpless, like sheep without a shepherd.
Matthew 9:36

There are gut-wrenching moments in life — the kind that hit you so hard it feels like someone is ripping your insides out.

Matthew suggests here Jesus experienced a gut-wrenching moment when he saw so many people beaten down by life, facing problems so overwhelming they didn't even know where to go for help.

In this moment, Jesus looked at his disciples and said, "I want your help with this. There are so many people who need relief — who need to know and experience God's compassion — that I need you to help me with this great harvest" (Matthew 9:37–38, author paraphrase).

Jesus calls us to join him in his work. He says, in effect, "I'm not going to keep doing this ministry by myself. I want you to be able to do it too. So come, work with me and see how God saturates us with his compassion."

Can You See It?

So we fix our eyes not on what is seen, but on what is unseen.
For what is seen is temporary, but what is unseen is eternal.
2 Corinthians 4:18

When life begins to squeeze us, what we truly believe is revealed through our attitudes and actions. And, the truth be told, most of us live by sight more than by the hope and certainty of our faith.

With the patience of Job, Jesus tells us again and again that we have to look past the things we see into the eternal reality of the unseen. The way to do that is to stay intimate with him and to let the Holy Spirit direct our sight, both our physical eyes and our spiritual eyes.

When we believe that reality is confined to only what we see, we become trapped into thinking truth is only what we see. We become prisoners to our perceptions; we cease to be freedom fighters walking in faith.

Our objective-in-Jesus is to grow confident in the truth that there is more to reality than what we see and that the spiritual realm is a genuine and essential part of our lives.

PUSHING EACH OTHER
TOWARD ONENESS

But encourage one another daily, as long as it is called Today,
so that none of you may be hardened by sin's deceitfulness.
Hebrews 3:13

We need Jesus-ones in our lives who love us enough to warn us when we are slipping in our faith. Just as "iron sharpens iron" (Proverbs 27:17), we push each other toward unity with God and the behavior born of such intimacy.

Our warnings should be positive and *redemptive*—calling each of us to a higher place and reminding one another of our godly purpose.

The Bible suggests that warnings motivated by love and based on committed relationships are less likely to come across as mean or harsh or cruelly critical (cf. 1 John 3:11–20). Instead, they are *exhortations for restoration* that indicate our love for others. They speak specifically about the depth of our love for them—that we love them enough to confront and exhort them to continue in their good fight of faith.

When you point out a blind spot, don't do it in anger. Your motive should be to restore your friend to a strong walk with Jesus. Ask yourself before speaking, "How can I make this warning tender?"

THE LORD OUR GOD,
THE LORD IS ONE

Love the LORD your God with all your heart
and with all your soul and with all your strength.
Deuteronomy 6:5

Truth says it's impossible to love God without first acknowledging his sovereignty; it's a nonnegotiable, no-skipping-allowed step toward loving him with all your heart, soul, strength, and mind.

You may be wondering what sovereignty has to do with loving God. Jesus says we show our love of God when we obediently submit to his sovereignty: "If anyone loves me, he will obey my teaching. My Father will love him, and we will come to him and make our home with him" (John 14:23).

This doesn't suggest God considers love a mere act of duty; rather it reveals his passion for oneness.

In the language of romance, we might say it this way: We are to love God so dearly that our hearts beat as one with his. Our agenda, our focus, and our desires become one with his, just as two newlyweds become one with each other.

Our objective-in-Jesus is to love God with heart, soul, strength, and mind, and we move toward that as we align our desires with his.

DEVELOPING DISCERNMENT

We have not received the spirit of the world but
the Spirit who is from God, that we may understand
what God has freely given us.
1 Corinthians 2:12

Sometimes you know something is true, even if the empirical evidence doesn't support what you know — *yet*. You could say you "know in your knower" it is true because the Spirit inside you is teaching you, by "expressing spiritual truths in spiritual words" (1 Corinthians 2:13).

God gives you spiritual discernment and that allows you to make spiritual judgments based on the truth of God's Word (1 Corinthians 2:11 – 16). You are no longer limited to seeing life, circumstances, or others from a mere human perspective; you can now see through the loving eyes of God (2 Corinthians 5:16).

Our objective-in-Jesus is to become confident of the Spirit's work within us, even when we cannot see it or feel it. We live by faith and not by sight.

TEMPTATION IS NOT A SIN

For we do not have a high priest who is unable to sympathize with our weaknesses, but we have one who has been tempted in every way, just as we are—yet was without sin.
Hebrews 4:15

If we believe temptation is sin, then we are more likely to give in to temptation, because we assume we have already crossed the line. But the Bible teaches temptation is not a sin. When Jesus was tempted, he still had not sinned (Hebrews 4:15).

The thought is not the sin. You can have the thought to steal the apple, but if you dismiss it immediately, sending it to the feet of King Jesus, then you still haven't sinned. Sin begins with the thought that *lingers*, leading to the question, "Did He really say we couldn't eat it?" Sin begins when you lust for the apple, fondling it with your eyes. Sin is when you eat it, even when you've been told to never do that.

When we are tempted, our objective-in-Jesus is to fight back by taking "captive every thought to make it obedient to Christ" (2 Corinthians 10:5). We stand firm against temptation by focusing on God and not on the sin that is singing seductively in our ears.

We are children of the almighty God, and by the blood of Jesus Christ, we are free to push away temptation and say no to sin.

No Longer by Instinct

But he denied it. "Woman, I don't know him," he said.
Luke 22:57

Peter gave in to fear when he knew he should have stood firm in faith. In realization of this he went out and wept bitterly (Luke 22:62).

Just as we often do, Peter followed his instincts for survival. He could not yet understand that the Holy Spirit would enter the lives of those who loved Jesus and create a direct and permanent connection between the Creator and the created.

Now, by teaching and guiding us, the Holy Spirit replaces our instincts; we no longer live by impulse and feeling, but by God's direct instruction. We may still make impulsive mistakes where we fall back into sinful patterns, but these are what Corrie ten Boom refers to as *echoes of the past*.

Years after the night when Peter stumbled in his faith, he wrote we are "a chosen people, a royal priesthood, a holy nation, a people belonging to God, that [we] may declare the praises of him who called [us] out of darkness into his wonderful light" (1 Peter 2:9).

As God's people, we now listen for God's voice and the promptings of the Holy Spirit.

An Inexhaustible Love

Because of the LORD's great love we are not consumed,
for his compassions never fail. They are new every morning;
great is your faithfulness.
Lamentations 3:22–23

God will supply more and more and more love today, tomorrow, and forever. The ancient poet-prophet Jeremiah says this merciful love from God never fails; it's like an inexhaustible supply of fresh, loving-compassion coffee each morning.

Since God's compassion starts fresh every morning, you will never reach a point where the supply is exhausted. This means you can never blow it so badly that God will abandon you. He is the God of second chances, who offers a hope that does not disappoint, because he has poured his love into our hearts and has given us the Holy Spirit (Romans 5:5).

God will make it so. The Hebrew word for faithfulness is related to the word *amen*, which means "so be it." When you close a prayer with amen, you are quite literally acknowledging that God is faithful to make it so. How would your prayers be different if you deeply believed God will make it so?

IF YOU WANT TO BE PERFECT

*"There is only One who is good. If you want to enter life,
obey the commandments."*
Matthew 19:17

The rich, young ruler came to Jesus with the question,
"Teacher, what good thing must I do to get eternal life?"
(Matthew 19:16). Mark says Jesus loved this man (Mark
10:21). Jesus was trying to bring the young man to the brink
of "I can't, but God can."

Pushing him closer to the edge of "I can't," Jesus said,
"If you're committed to earn your way into eternal life, then
be absolutely perfect" (Matthew 19:21, author paraphrase).
And what did Jesus mean by this? The ruler would have to
be better than the Pharisees and the teachers of the law (cf.
Matthew 5:20).

Jesus looked into the man and pointed out what was most
likely making him cling to "I can." His wealth was keeping
him independent from God; he relied on his wealth more
than he relied on God.

We may not be wealthy, but when Jesus looks into us, he
will point out the one thing that is keeping us from depending
completely on God. What could that one thing be in you?

TRUTH: GOD'S LOVE FILLS ME

*May the grace of the Lord Jesus Christ, and the love of God,
and the fellowship of the Holy Spirit be with you all.*
2 Corinthians 13:14

In faith, I know these things to be true:

- God is full of love and grace, and he fills me with his love and grace.
- God's work within me is to clear a channel for his love and grace to flow through me into the lives of anyone and everyone I meet.
- I may not be there yet, but I am "confident of this, that he who began a good work in [me] will carry it on to completion until the day of Christ Jesus" (Philippians 1:6).
- Through the "Lord Jesus Christ, and the love of God, and the fellowship of the Holy Spirit," I am, at all times, filled with grace, mercy, and peace (2 Corinthians 13:14).

This is what I believe to be true and I will walk accordingly. Father, I believe; help my unbelief (cf. Mark 9:24).

BE UN-CONFORMED

Do not conform any longer to the pattern of this world,
but be transformed by the renewing of your mind.
Romans 12:2

Slowly read through this devotional as a prayer to God:

Lord, transform my mind so that I no longer conform to this age, but un-conform to anything that is not a part of you or pleasing to you.

Renew my mind so I am transformed by your power. Develop my ability to discern your will and energize me to do things that are pleasing to you.

Father, I pray this prayer for my family, that we will no longer be so "well-adjusted to [our] culture that [we] fit into it without even thinking" (Romans 12:2 MSG). We want to be God-adjusted within the culture of our home, neighborhood, and community.

Lord, help us to drop the weapons of the flesh we still wield when we feel threatened or confused. Teach us to pick up and use the many weapons of the Spirit you provide.

We are your sons and daughters; re-create us into fathers and mothers of the faith.

A WHOLE HEART: MIND

"Love the Lord your God ... with all your mind."
Luke 10:27b

To love God with your whole mind requires you to think like God. It means your thoughts start to match God's thoughts and your perspective about people and situations starts to match God's perspective.

Thinking like God means:

- You trust his guidance and no longer rely on your own understanding.
- You allow God to interpret the facts, since he knows the whole truth.
- You measure your thoughts against God's Word and God's character.
- You take ungodly thoughts captive and bring them before King Jesus.

You will not be able to change the way you think without God's help, but this dependence on him brings you to a place of strength, not weakness. The only reason your thoughts are not one with God is because you are thinking independent of the mind of Christ (1 Corinthians 2:16).

Your Guide for Life's Journey

But when he, the Spirit of truth, comes,
he will guide you into all truth.
John 16:13

God wants you to trust his guidance, so he sent you a Guide.

The Holy Spirit is your Guide, one who walks with you along the way. He knows every step of the journey and understands the blessings and dangers ahead. He knows where you've been and where you're going, and he knows the best path to take.

This is important to understand because God never intended for you to figure out the steps of your journey without him. Your responsibility is to seek his guidance and obey his directions.

God says, "I will instruct you and teach you in the way you should go; I will counsel you and watch over you" (Psalm 32:8).

You don't have to know the reason for everything, and there's no requirement that you figure it all out before you begin your mission. You just need to trust and obey.

Ask God to show you places where you may be attempting a self-guided tour as opposed to relying on the experienced Guide, the Holy Spirit, for your journey.

No Commandment Was Harmed

For these rules are only shadows of the reality yet to come.
And Christ himself is that reality.
Colossians 2:17 (NLT)

Grace straps us to the law of love, binding us with the Holy Spirit to the life of Christ.

Some may think a focus on grace downgrades the law, but authentic grace agrees with God's assessment that sin is so huge it can only be rendered powerless with a bloody blow from the Lord resurrected.

Grace cost Jesus his life, but it places the life of Christ in us, which compels us to give our lives, based on God's grace, to others.

God's grace is never cheap, writes Dietrich Bonhoeffer: "It is costly because it costs a man his life, and it is grace because it gives a man the only true life. It is costly because it condemns sin, and grace because it justifies the sinner."

God doesn't give us grace so that we will continue to sin; he gives us grace so we are free not to sin. No commandment is harmed when we live by God's grace.

By embracing grace, we accept the responsibility to maintain a close communion with God through the Holy Spirit. And if we are led by the Spirit, we are no longer under law (Galatians 5:18).

DOES LOVE DANCE IN YOUR EYES?

*"I remember the devotion of your youth, how as a bride you
loved me and followed me through the desert."*
Jeremiah 2:2

The word devotion in Jeremiah 2:2 is a translation of
the Hebrew word *chesed*, which is often translated as "loving
mercy" or "loving kindness." It is a love of relentless pursuit, and throughout the Bible, it shows up like mile-markers
measuring God's grace-chase after his prodigal sons and
daughters, refusing to let them get away from the mercy of
his love.

But something surprised me in these prophetic words
from Jeremiah. In a sense, God says, "I remember the devoted,
loyal love of your youth. You were like a new bride with love
dancing in your eyes, and you'd follow me through the desert
or into a desolate land."

In effect God says, "I remember your youth, when *you*
chased after me with all your heart, soul, strength, and mind."
If you once chased after God with every bit of your being, it
is possible to do it again.

God says we are capable of giving him our whole love. If
he says we can, why do we say we can't?

NEVER SAY AMEN

Then he returned to his disciples and found them sleeping.
"Could you men not keep watch with me
for one hour?" he asked Peter.
Matthew 26:40

Read this devotional as a prayer:

Help me, Lord, to develop a strong prayer life. I know you desire intimacy with me, yet, I often fail to find the time to pray. What draws me to my knees is when I have a problem, when I want something from you, when I need your help.

Help me turn my prayers into conversations with you that keep flowing throughout the day—ongoing communication, in which I never say amen.

Keep me close to you, no matter what it takes, so I can become one with your heart.

I pray that you will create me worthy of my calling and that your power will fulfill every good purpose you plan for me and will energize everything I do in faith.

My prayer is that your life will appear in my smile, in my hands, in my thoughts, and in my words. I know your grace will make it so (2 Thessalonians 1:11–12).

JESUS-LOVE IS PERSONAL

We are from God, and whoever knows God listens to us ...
This is how we recognize the Spirit of truth
and the spirit of falsehood.
1 John 4:6

My mother gave me a great gift of sensitivity when giving. I see giving as an opportunity to show I have thought about the likes and needs of someone else. The fact that there are so many returns after Christmas and so many gift cards purchased shows we are not taking the time to make gifts personal.

Just like gifts, love operates personally. Jesus came to bring us into the personal embrace of a passionate and loving relationship with him.

We live in an increasingly impersonal world where a phone call usually leads to a recorded message and emails often arrive from people working twenty feet away from us. We live as if the Internet somehow replaces our desperate need for deep, transparent, authentic, personal relationships.

Yet, we are from God, the Creator and Protector of all that is personal. When we *personalize* our love, we proclaim: "Do you want to see how God personally loves us? Watch how we love one another."

An Image of Perfect Love

God spoke: "Let us make human beings in our image,
make them reflecting our nature."
Genesis 1:26 (MSG)

God the Father, Son, and Spirit are the original small group. The Trinity is a never-beginning, never-ending community where there is intimacy, harmony, fellowship, and friendship.

In this Trinitarian community, we see the blueprint for authentic community: all have equal value, each looks out for the other, one is ever ready to sacrifice for the sake of someone else, and everyone is absolutely safe. It's a community of fearlessness, a fully free and uninhibited expression of godly love.

We are made in the image of this perfect love (Genesis 1:26), created as a race of beings to love and to be loved. We are designed to be at home in God's perfect love and to be cocreators of a loving community on earth, where human lives are personally and purposefully shaped.

"Since God so loved us, we also ought to love one another" (1 John 4:11). Our objective-in-Jesus is to become part of a transparent, authentic Christ-community, trusting God's love is stronger than our fears.

WE CARRY CHRIST'S DEATH

Not that I have already obtained all this, or have already
been made perfect, but I press on to take hold of that
for which Christ Jesus took hold of me.
Philippians 3:12

My friend Nancy Guthrie once said, "When you're in the middle of a crisis, you'd like to think God would give you a pass on the everyday problems." At the time, Nancy's daughter had just been diagnosed with Zellweger syndrome and had only a few months to live.

Yet, within her heartache, I saw Nancy move deeper and deeper into the heart of God. She and her husband did not dwell on the question, "Why us?" Instead, they began to ask, "God, what do you want to do with this circumstance?"

God uses our tragedies like an involuntary surgery that causes fear and even greater pain, but on the other side we are stronger, on the way to recovery from our disease of faithlessness. Even though it may be difficult to see how God can do that, or even to see God at work, you will grow more confident that he is moving you toward a peaceful future (Jeremiah 29:11; Romans 8:28).

Jesus Is Discipleship

Now you've got my feet on the life path,
all radiant from the shining of your face. Ever since
you took my hand, I'm on the right way.
Psalm 16:11 (MSG)

Jesus does not show us the way; he is the way (John 14:6).

- If we want to learn about God, we go to Jesus.
- If we want to learn how to live a life pleasing to God, we go to Jesus.
- If we want to learn about love, we go to Jesus.
- If we want to know Jesus, we go to Jesus

All discipleship eventually leads back to Jesus, who is not only our Master and Teacher; he is also the curriculum we learn from. We mature as we "grow up into" Jesus (Ephesians 4:15).

"We don't have to rely on the world's guesses and opinions," says Paul, the apostle. "We didn't learn this by reading books or going to school; we learned it from God, who taught us person-to-person through Jesus, and we're passing it on to you in the same firsthand, personal way" (1 Corinthians 2:13 MSG).

"Prideligion"

*They crush people with unbearable religious demands
and never lift a finger to ease the burden.*
Matthew 23:4 (NLT)

We are surprisingly tolerant of a heretical form of religion, a religion of pride or perhaps the pride of religion — "prideligion," if you will.

Prideligion is prevalent among people who live according to lists of their own making. Lists make us feel like we are accomplishing something. They make us feel proud that we are able to do everything on the list, that we are bringing our holiness to God.

There is nothing wrong with establishing goals in discipleship, but the problem occurs when we let our lists of what a believer "ought" to do and "ought" to say replace our relationship with God.

Lists can crush us with "unbearable religious demands" (Matthew 23:4 NLT). They put us in danger of becoming dependent on them, thereby derailing our desire to remain dependent on the Father, the ruler over all lists.

Our objective-in-Jesus is to develop a Christ-walk that shows others "love is the fulfillment of the law" (Romans 13:10).

OBJECTIVE-IN-JESUS:
SEE PAST THE SIN

*We who are strong ought to bear with the failings
of the weak and not to please ourselves.*
Romans 15:1

When we see someone straying from the faith, instead of judging him, our objective is to try to understand the reason for his drift. Then we need to be ready to address the needs and concerns God reveals to us.

Both Paul and James teach that those living in the Spirit are to pursue and restore those who have slipped back into living the old, worldly ways, once abandoned for Christ (Romans 14–15; Galatians 6; James 5). "Each one of us needs to look after the good of the people around us, asking ourselves, 'How can I help?'" (Romans 15:1–2 MSG).

We encourage people to accept their individuality (to be themselves) and yet reject individualism (living for themselves). It is this kind of acceptance—the same way Christ accepted us—that encourages us toward spiritual maturity. When we look past the faults of others and, instead, offer them acceptance, we reflect the heart of Jesus and encourage godly growth.

GOD OF ALL COMFORT

Praise be to ... the God of all comfort, who comforts us in all our troubles, so that we can comfort those in any trouble with the comfort we ourselves have received from God.

2 Corinthians 1:3–4

God, who is omnipotent, sees the breadth and depth of our circumstances, and he knows his plans for our lives. Thinking like Christ, we can slowly begin to understand that avoiding the pain in our lives is actually an *act of faithlessness*.

Standing firm in our faith allows us to respond to God instead of reacting to our difficult circumstances. It helps us grow confident in the truth that God is our strength for enduring any problems we face.

Our objective-in-Jesus is to move toward the place where we are able to ask God, "What do you want me to do with this?" instead of falling into a "Why me?" trap.

Ultimately, we move toward the other-centered love we are learning from Jesus, with a growing certainty that our experience with problems and pain, and just the plain mess of life, will give us the ability to comfort others when they are facing similar circumstances.

BLESSED BY INADEQUACY

Let him who boasts boast in the Lord.
1 Corinthians 1:31

You are not the only believer to feel inadequate for service and mission. The apostle Paul encouraged some of the first Christians with these words: "Think of what you were when you were called. Not many of you were wise by human standards; not many were influential; not many were of noble birth. But God chose the foolish things of the world to shame the wise; God chose the weak things of the world to shame the strong" (1 Corinthians 1:26–27).

But your feelings of inadequacy have no bearing on the truth: God is adequate for the task, and he will energize you with the adequacy of the Holy Spirit within you. You can do all things through him who strengthens you (Philippians 4:13).

This means you cannot fail in your service to God; and when your service helps others, you can boast in the Lord instead of your own abilities and resources.

Instead of being overwhelmed by the giants before us, be overwhelmed by God's mighty power and awesomeness. Like Paul, be overwhelmed with God's joy; like Peter, be overwhelmed by God's wonder. We can say, like the boy David said to the giant Goliath, "You come against me with sword and spear and javelin, but I come against you in the name of the LORD Almighty" (1 Samuel 17:45).

A Saint Birthed by Trials

We are hard pressed on every side, but not crushed;
perplexed, but not in despair; persecuted, but not abandoned;
struck down, but not destroyed.
2 Corinthians 4:8–9

When we confess our belief in Jesus as the Holy One of God, we often assume our lives will become easier.

Jesus taught that his yoke is easy (Matthew 11:30) and Paul spoke about the Sabbath rest of God (Hebrews 4:9), but both these examples teach the need to develop a deep trust in God — not that following Jesus is easy. We are to step into the will of God and stay there, trusting that he has our best interests at heart (Jeremiah 29:11; Romans 8:28).

Yet, the deeper we head into God's heart, the more difficult things are likely to become as God builds a Jesus-like character within us.

We want to make a significant contribution to the kingdom of God, but at the same time, we want to sidestep the trails God uses to grow us as saints. Instead of asking, "Why me?" when you are suffering, ask God to show you what to do with the tragedy. He is well aware of your struggle and he is not surprised or offended when you express you anger or frustration, even if it is aimed at him.

THE WITNESS FROM WITHIN

*The Spirit himself testifies with our spirit
that we are God's children.*
Romans 8:16

You're sitting in a restaurant where an older man gets a bit cantankerous and his conversation, although not loud, lets negativity creep into the dining room.

Just then, Mrs. Jones and some of her friends are seated. They are in a festive mood, laughing, hugging, and cheerfully greeting diners around their table.

Their joy spills across the room, changing the entire atmosphere—even the cantankerous old man is now smiling and laughing; it leaves you longing to be part of their group.

Mrs. Jones is a snapshot of ourselves when we let the perfect love of God drive the fear from our lives (1 John 4:18). It is then that God's Spirit in us testifies with our spirit that we are God's children (Romans 8:15–16). And the joy of Jesus working within us bubbles out as an unforced testimony of God's life in us.

Embrace God's grace until the love and joy you experience is infectious, spreading to those around you, creating a longing within them to join the family of God.

DISHWASHER DIALOGUE

So whether you eat or drink or whatever you do,
do it all for the glory of God.
1 Corinthians 10:31

My wife is a dishwasher organizer. The dishes are placed according to size and the silverware is positioned to receive the most efficient cleaning. I take the free-form approach: that is, if it's in the machine somewhere, somehow, then surely (hopefully) it will get clean.

These conflicting styles have led to what my sweet southern aunt calls "lively discussions." The next time you engage in a dishwasher dialogue (or any sort of lively discussion), recall the apostle Paul and his radical explanation that worship — your intimacy with God — should saturate the most mundane moments of your life.

Simple acts of living become acts of worship when done according to God's purpose and pleasure. For instance, you will need more faith to worship God when your spouse loads the dishwasher wrong (*again*) than the faith required to worship God in the sanctuary this weekend.

We become living sacrifices, not by becoming nice, but by sacrificing our desires to work independently and allowing God to work through us.

Enjoy the "Happy Cake"

Celebrate God all day, every day. I mean, revel in him!
Philippians 4:4 (MSG)

My son, Christopher, was captivated by birthdays when he was young. His joy overflowed when he saw a "happy cake."

Sometimes he would spontaneously designate someone as the birthday boy or girl and start singing the "Happy Birthday" song. I never failed to see such a birthday-designee light up like a candle on a cake. My son's celebration of each life was infectious; it ministered to everyone Christopher celebrated in song.

You too can serve others simply by celebrating their lives when you let them know how much you appreciate them, when you let them know they are accepted by you and by God, and when you let them know they are important and uniquely designed by God.

This Jesus-joy in you will bring Jesus-joy to others. So, let me start with you: You are a sweet fragrance to God. He loves you and it brings him great joy when he thinks of you. He celebrates your life, and he wants you to join the festivities.

Shhh ... listen carefully ... is that someone singing "Happy Birthday" to you?

GRACE IS GREATER THAN SIN

*Do not cast me from your presence or take
your Holy Spirit from me.*
Psalm 51:11

Do you ever fear God will banish you from his presence? That you've gone one step beyond God's patience and grace?

King David, of ancient Israel, expressed a similar concern. But he ran like a man chasing after God's own heart straight into the unlimited grace of God, a grace rooted in a perfect love that casts out all fear (1 John 4:18).

David understood that God brings holiness to us; we don't become holy to reach him. God's grace, flowing from the blood of Jesus Christ, allows us to boldly approach God (Hebrews 4:16) and no longer fear banishment or abandonment. We are joyfully accepted as beloved children (Ephesians 1:5), now and forever (Romans 8:35, 39).

The really, really, good, good news is this: God's grace is greater than Adam's fall; his grace is greater than your greatest sin; his grace is greater than all your sins combined; and his grace will keep you in his presence, even when you think you are unworthy. Pray, "Lord, I (want to) believe; help my unbelief."

GOD SEES WHO?

The LORD turned to [Gideon] and said,
"Go in the strength you have and save Israel out of
Midian's hand. Am I not sending you?"
Judges 6:14

Gideon was the least member of the weakest clan in the tribe of Manasseh. On the day in question he was doing the tedious task of threshing wheat.

God saw Gideon as a mighty warrior and judge who would lead the Israelites back to their proper worship of God (Judges 6:12). Gideon, however, saw himself as just a guy cranking out wheat in a creaky old winepress.

But this didn't matter to God. He told Gideon: "Go in the strength you have and save Israel out of Midian's hand. Am I not sending you?" (Judges 6:14).

It doesn't matter what Gideon says about himself or what others say about Gideon. Only one opinion counts: God's. What God says about Gideon is the truth; what God says about you is also the truth.

FORGETTING FAITH

So I will always remind you of these things,
even though you know them and are firmly
established in the truth you now have.
2 Peter 1:12

At one point when trying to live like Jesus, I sensed God telling me to stop receiving a regular paycheck and start living "on faith."

So, with certainty that God would provide because he told me he would, I did what he said and started looking for his provision. I even kept a log of every way that God took care of us. God was moving me from a tentative "I hope it will happen" to a certain "I know this will happen."

But within a few months I lost my focus on God, and I started scrambling for ways to generate income, believing, again, that it was my responsibility to make things happen. Could it be that I forgot what I believed? C. S. Lewis, in *Mere Christianity*, says people are never talked out of their faith, but they may slowly, imperceptibly at first, forget what they believe.

Peter says we should keep our memories fresh, so that we are constantly encouraged by the truth of God's work in our lives.

SENSING GOD'S PLEASURE

"I have given them the glory that you gave me, that they may be one as we are one: I in them and you in me."
John 17:22–23

We worship God by the way we live (Romans 12). This allows our Creator to give us intimate insight into why he was pleased to create us as he did. Olympic gold medalist Eric Liddell describes it best: "When I run, I feel God's pleasure."

There are things you were created to do, and when you do them, you bring God pleasure. It is an act of worship and praise and thanks for the gifts God has given you. These connections take us straight to the heart of God, allowing us to sense his heartbeat and to share a part of his joy. They are a constant reminder that God is in heaven, God knows us by name, and God is bringing us home to him.

Think about your gifts and abilities. Which ones seem to bring you into the very presence of God when you use them? This is an act of worship. Use them as often as possible.

GOD USES FAMILY TO MATURE YOU

So Joseph also went up ... He went there to register with Mary, who was pledged to be married to him and was expecting a child.
Luke 2:4–5

God uses your family to direct you toward his purpose. The family into which you were born was not the result of an accident; God spoke you, quite deliberately, into your mother's womb.

Jesus had a family too. We tend to think of his family in big picture terms — that he had a heavenly Father, that he was the son of the Virgin Mary, or that he was an heir to David's throne. But Jesus had a flesh and blood family, and God used that family to move Jesus toward his holy purpose, including his birth in Bethlehem.

God has placed you in your family to help you become a masterpiece, a portrait of Jesus. Hopefully, your character will grow into one like Christ's, with the help of positive role models who will encourage and support your spiritual growth.

And, if you are in a difficult family situation, God will still use your family as an instrument that transforms you into a person like Jesus. He works all things together for good (Romans 8:28).

Is God Keeping You from Getting What You Want?

Now the serpent ... said to the woman, "Did God really say,
'You must not eat from any tree in the garden'?"
Genesis 3:1

Waiting is the hardest part, and Sarai was tired of waiting. She took it upon herself to fulfill God's promise, no longer trusting the Almighty to do his job (Genesis 16).

Perhaps she heard a voice like the hiss of a serpent, saying, "Did God really say your husband would be the father of a family so vast it would surpass the number of stars in the sky?"

Perhaps Sarai said, "God can, but he won't." Or maybe she said, "God can't figure this out, but I can."

Sarai believed her assumptions more than she believed God's promise. She wondered why God was no longer on her side, instead of confessing that she was no longer one with God's will.

Ask God to help you identify the places in your life where you are saying, "The Lord is keeping this from me!" God will continue to teach you—and stretch you—until walking by faith and not by sight is as natural as breathing.

IN STEP WITH THE SPIRIT

Since we live by the Spirit, let us keep in step with the Spirit.
Galatians 5:25

When we ignore the Holy Spirit, there is little difference between the way we live our lives and the way unbelievers live—their lives disconnected and independent from God.

Our objective is to become sensitive to the Holy Spirit. Ask God to teach you to hear his still small voice and to be sensitive to promptings from the Spirit that he has placed inside you. Then, believe the truth that he will guide you through the decisions and details of your life.

For the next few weeks, list all the times you sense the Spirit prompting you. This will help you learn to be sensitive to the Spirit and will strengthen your resolve to be obedient to God's guidance as you see his constant, loving interest in the details of your life.

And what if you blow it? Remember God's grace! If you misunderstand the Holy Spirit's prompting or disobey it, confess your failure to God; he is faithful to forgive (1 John 1:9).

A DIVINE DEFENSE

"You come against me with sword and spear and javelin,
but I come against you in the name of the LORD Almighty."
1 Samuel 17:45

During World War II, the B-17 bomber was known as the flying fortress because it carried thirteen .50 caliber machine guns.

Scientific testing suggested that without the weight of the guns, the planes could fly faster and higher, increasing the chance of survival during daylight missions. But the pilots said there was no way they were going on a mission without the guns. They wanted to be able to shoot back.

We make the same choice in our battles. God tells us we don't need weapons of the flesh; we can soar higher and faster with him and his weapons of the Spirit. But we say, "No thanks, we have to shoot back!" We defend ourselves with angry words, manipulative maneuvers, and bombs of blame.

It takes faith to stop using these weapons of the flesh and instead arm ourselves with the weapons of God. Our objective-in-Jesus is to grow confident in the truth that God is "a shield to those who take refuge in him" (Proverbs 30:5).

A Spiritual Legacy

The things which you have heard from me in the presence
of many witnesses, entrust these to faithful men
who will be able to teach others also.
2 Timothy 2:2 (NASB)

God designed you so that your life will have meaning beyond your days on earth. You are meant to leave a Jesus-legacy with those around you.

Even if you are a new believer, or if you are the first person in your family to become a believer, you already have a deep and rich spiritual heritage in Jesus, who was the first in a long legacy of those who will be raised from the dead.

This heritage is a trust of God's great truths that you should guard carefully and then intentionally pass on to others. If you fail to guard the truths, the legacy may become polluted with false ideas about God; and if you fail to pass the truths on to others, your godly heritage may stop with you.

God entrusted you to do this, and he will energize you to do this; you cannot fail. Our objective-in-Jesus is to intentionally pass what we know about Jesus on to others, encouraging them to pass on the same teachings to others, and on and on.

BLIND TRUTH: JESUS SENT

So the man went and washed, and came home seeing.
John 9:7–8

At first, the blind man may have hesitated, confused about how going to Siloam would give him sight. He may have been wondering, "Why would Jesus make me do this when he could have simply healed me back there?"

He may have heard the laughter and ridicule as people watched him slowly walk toward the pool: "Look at that fool with the mud on his face." "Are you crazy enough to think you'll really be healed?"

But the blind man could not be shamed from doing whatever it took to be healed. Jesus told him what to do, and that's what he would do, no matter what anyone else said.

Do what Jesus tells you to do. Jesus gave the blind man his sight, and his experience shows that Jesus uses our obedience to heal our hurts and to strengthen our faith.

Do exactly what Jesus says to do. When Jesus tells us what to do, we need to pay close attention to the details. He may be asking more than you think, but listen carefully—he may be asking you to do less than you assume.

Blessed Peacemakers
Bless Others

"Blessed are the peacemakers,
for they will be called sons of God."
Matthew 5:9

With every step I take today, I proclaim the good news of peace with God (Ephesians 6:15).

Wherever I go, I am a peacemaker. I help others make peace with God and make peace with one another. I am able to tell everyone I meet — sometimes even using words — that God is the source of my peace: "For he himself is our peace, who has made the two one and has destroyed the barrier, the dividing wall of hostility" (Ephesians 2:14).

We proclaim that we can rest peacefully in God's hands, knowing "neither death nor life, neither angels nor demons, neither the present nor the future, nor any powers, neither height nor depth, nor anything else in all creation, will be able to separate us from the love of God that is in Christ Jesus our Lord" (Romans 8:38 – 39).

Our objective-in-Jesus is to become lights of peace, no longer hidden but shining from "a city on a hill." Therefore, "in the same way, let your light shine before men, that they may see your good deeds and praise your Father in heaven" (Matthew 5:14, 16).

CARRY EACH OTHER'S BURDENS

Carry each other's burdens,
and in this way you will fulfill the law of Christ.
Galatians 6:2

We are to help our brothers and sisters carry the heavy burdens of life—a terrible loss, a crushing circumstance, a painful diagnosis—the kinds of troubles that threaten to overwhelm and destroy us, similar to the pressing weight of the cross that Jesus carried to Golgotha (John 19:17).

Like Simon from Cyrene, who shouldered the heavy wooden cross with Jesus (Mark 15:21), we are to step in with support for our friends, even if that means we carry their burden for a while.

Our acts of love and support as we help each other face the troubles in our homes, our careers, our marriages, and with our health complete this "law of Christ." We build our lives on the promise of the Father, who will never leave or forsake us (Deuteronomy 31:6), and we offer that same promise to our families and friends.

The worst thing we can do when we are going through a crisis is to isolate ourselves. We need others to help us carry our burdens and to offer us support, encouragement, and simply their presence (Proverbs 18:24).

CHASING AMBULANCES

So the law was put in charge to lead us to Christ
that we might be justified by faith.
Galatians 3:24

I recently read about a state enacting a law requiring motorists to pull over when an emergency vehicle passes with lights on and sirens blaring.

Pulling aside for emergency vehicles should be ingrained in us, but I've noticed that more drivers seem reluctant to do so. Maybe we are less concerned about following the law. Or, maybe it's because we've become so busy and self-absorbed we don't want to be inconvenienced by slowing down. So a rule that used to be "in our hearts" now requires a written law in order to get everyone to comply.

God had to do the same thing. He designed us to live by his Spirit; but because we refused to comply, God sent us legislation — starting with the Ten Commandments — to push us toward holy living.

God wants you to operate in such a way that you don't need legislation (or willpower, or guilt) to force you to follow the rules because the rules are written on your heart by the very hand of God.

FALSE GUILT AND CONDEMNATION

If the old covenant, which brings condemnation,
was glorious, how much more glorious is the new covenant,
which makes us right with God!
2 Corinthians 3:9 (NLT, 1996 ed.)

Lord, the air is swirling with false guilt and whispered condemnation, even within the community of believers.

What we have done wrong has been forgiven; yet, we still feel the weight of condemnation. But you, Lord, do not condemn. So the condemnation must be coming from the enemy, and he has no authority to condemn us.

You are our advocate, sitting at the right hand of God, telling the Father that you have covered our sins and cleansed us white as snow.

Sweep away this rubble of false guilt, clearing a path for mercy, grace, love, and acceptance.

Jesus, we know your desire for us is freedom, the freedom you paid so steep a price to purchase for us and to give us freely. We receive this freedom from condemnation, Lord, and we thank you for this gift.

FORM LETTERS TO GOD

The heart is deceitful above all things and beyond cure.
Who can understand it?
Jeremiah 17:9

There is a story of a businessman who climbs into bed at a hotel only to find it full of bugs. When the man gets home, he writes a letter of complaint to the hotel's corporate headquarters.

Weeks later, he receives a reply directly from the president of the company apologizing for the incident and promising to rectify the problem. The businessman feels great! The hotel management has heard him, they are committed to making a change, and now every customer will benefit from his initiative. As he folds the letter, a small Post-it note floats to the floor that says, "Send this guy the bug letter."

Have you been sending "bug letters" to God? Standardized responses to God's commands, directions, or promptings that allow you to walk by sight and not by faith?

It's easy to say you will be a more supportive husband and a more attentive father, or a more loving mother and a more encouraging wife. Will you allow God to lead your transformation, or will you simply send him a form letter?

GIVE ME A HEAD WITH HAIR

But because of his great love for us, God, who is rich in mercy,
made us alive with Christ even when we were dead in
transgressions — it is by grace you have been saved.
Ephesians 2:4 – 5

Back when I had a full head of hair, a group called the Cowsills sang: "Give me a head with hair, long beautiful hair."

Today a major issue among men is whether or not they have hair. *USA Today* reports that in 2006 over $1.2 billion was spent worldwide for hair-restoration surgeries. Science is now reaching a new breakthrough — the ability to transplant an entire scalp, as in a head full of hair from a dead man onto the head of a living man.

What does this have to do with your Jesus-life?

My hope is it will help you remember this truth: We are dead to our old, pre-Jesus life and have been raised to a new life in Christ (Romans 6:4 – 5). We have no need of a life-transplant because we are new creations in Christ: "the old has gone, the new has come!" (2 Corinthians 5:17).

GOD IS ABLE

"No eye has seen, no ear has heard, no mind has conceived
what God has prepared for those who love him."
1 Corinthians 2:9

God is sovereign and that means he is able. He is able to take what you give and use it for his glory far beyond anything you could imagine (1 Corinthians 2:9).

God spoke the world into existence, and with the same power and creativity he spoke you into your mother's womb, timing your conception perfectly so that you would be here "for such a time as this" (Esther 4:14), the time predetermined for you to fulfill God's purpose.

You may feel inadequate to be part of God's plan, but he created you exactly how he wants you to be. Is it possible God knows more about your abilities than you do? Is it probable God would ask you to do things he never designed you to do, or without providing you with everything you need?

If God believes in you, is it possible that not believing in yourself is a subtle form of arrogance? Or devilish disobedience?

GOD OR MYTH?

"O Lord, the great and awesome God, who keeps his covenant of love with all who love him and obey his commands."
Daniel 9:4

Sovereignty simply means God has the right to rule; submission means we agree we have no right to rule. When we ignore God's sovereignty, we end up living in a mythological universe where we are lower-lords ruling feudal lands and we worship the little gods of independence and self-reliance.

When we say, "I can make this happen without you, God," we steal God's right to rule, like Promethean protégés intent on outwitting the Almighty. We think we are stealing sovereignty only to find that our mythology is a lie, one that smells of evil embers from hell.

We cannot live like Jesus alone, independent of God. When we abandon our mythology and submit to the sovereignty of God, only then do we become fully human, energized by the Holy Spirit to face our fears and to bring comfort to the world.

God's truth cannot allow any mythology to masquerade as reality. Our objective-in-Jesus is to eliminate the myths we live by; we are most likely to find those myths hidden beneath our worries and doubts.

God's Plan: A Hopeful Future

*"For I know the plans I have for you," says the LORD.
"They are plans for good and not for disaster,
to give you a future and a hope."*
Jeremiah 29:11 (NLT)

Why, God, do you allow bad things to happen?

When we are in the middle of a mess, we often quote Jeremiah 29:11. God is telling us that we may misunderstand and incorrectly perceive his plans as evil, but those plans are the very thing that will give us, literally, "a hopeful future."

God is pushing us toward a hopeful future, one where we are healed, where our burdens and mistakes are lifted from our shoulders, where we walk in the light of God's cleansing grace.

Ask God to help you develop a "hopeful future" faith, where, regardless of how bad things *appear*, you are *confident* God is working it for good.

IMAGE MANAGEMENT

*... so that you may become blameless and pure, children of God
without fault in a crooked and depraved generation,
in which you shine like stars in the universe.*
Philippians 2:15

We sin when we maneuver and posture to make our jars of clay look better; we decorate the outside with ecclesiastical vainglories that we call image, power, position, or wealth.

We do this because we think our power, which is easily surpassed, somehow makes us strong, when all the while it is in our weakness that God shows himself the strongest. His light shines through even greater as we acknowledge we can't do anything without him, but through him, all things are possible

The glory that shines from within us is not our own; it is God's glory and his alone. He is glorified as he re-creates his creations into blameless and pure children "without fault in a crooked and depraved generation, in which you shine like stars in the universe" (Philippians 2:15).

You, my friend, magnify the glory of God by simply being you and letting him shine through you. May God "make his face shine upon you and be gracious to you" (Numbers 6:25).

IMPERFECT DISHARMONY

May the God who gives endurance and encouragement
give you a spirit of unity among yourselves as you follow
Christ Jesus, so that with one heart and mouth you may
glorify the God and Father of our Lord Jesus Christ.
Romans 15:5–6

Spiritual disharmony can unsettle both individual and congregational worship. Jesus considered our unity with one another so critical that he said you should stop worship and go set things right with anyone who is at odds with you (Matthew 5:23). "Then and only then, come back and work things out with God" (Matthew 5:24 MSG).

What if we agreed not to have worship services until everyone in the congregation had set things right with each other? How quickly would conflicts be resolved?

If you are in conflict with someone, your mind is likely mulling over the person your heart is bitter toward—you are not ready to worship God. When you come to a worship service, your objective is to be able to tell God three things:

- I am coming to focus on you, God, not anything else.
- I am coming to offer praise from my heart and to use my gifts, talents, and abilities to worship you.
- I am coming to give, not to receive. My desire is to seek your face, not what is in your hand.

JESUS AND THE JERKS

But God demonstrates His own love toward us,
in that while we were yet sinners, Christ died for us.
Romans 5:8 (NASB)

One of the biggest jerks I ever knew was a twenty-three-year-old college graduate whose anger and arrogance spilled into many of his relationships. His hypocrisy was astounding as he claimed to be a Christian one moment and then acted like a son of hell the next. If it had been my choice, I would have avoided him all together, but that jerk was *me*.

Most of us try to avoid jerks, but Jesus embraced them; he graced them with love. He voluntarily stretched out his arms on the cross and allowed a few jerks to slam nails into his hands and feet.

Behind all their stomp and snort, jerks are still spiritual beings, created in God's image and destined for heaven or hell. We are compelled to be ministers of reconciliation, willing to embrace the pain of a fallen world for the sake of our God (2 Corinthians 5:16–21).

The heart of the gospel is that God loves the unlovely. Could it be that God places jerks in our lives to teach us to be more like Jesus, who loved the unlovely?

Jesus: New Wine for New Wineskins

"No one pours new wine into old wineskins.
If he does, the wine will burst the skins ...
No, he pours new wine into new wineskins."
Mark 2:22

Over the years, I've been in a lot of church meetings and ministry settings where the image of new wineskins flows as freely as Kool-Aid at vacation Bible school. The new wineskins concept is often applied to church structure and programs, plans, and priorities.

But I rarely hear the concept of new wineskins applied to a life, as in yours or mine. Don't we often try to put new wine into old wineskins when it comes to our Christian walk? What I mean is this: a new wine of "honesty at work" poured into an old wineskin of "cutting corners."

Here's the point: God pours the new wine of the Holy Spirit into the new wineskin of our new-creation lives, setting us steady on our kingdom walk. But we often reach into the discard pile and pull out our old wineskin, trying to make it work as part of our new life in Christ.

JESUS WAS A SEEKER

"For I have not come to call the righteous, but sinners."
Matthew 9:13

Jesus sought the lost.

You could say he was the original seeker, but unlike the modern term, Jesus didn't wait for seekers to seek him; he actively and sacrificially sought them.

When the Pharisees saw Jesus keeping company with "a lot of disreputable characters ... they had a fit, and lit into Jesus' followers. 'What kind of example is this from your Teacher, acting cozy with crooks and riff-raff?'" (Matthew 9:10–11 MSG).

They viewed Jesus as a bad example because he associated with people who needed God, who needed mercy, who thought they were beyond ever being accepted by God.

The Pharisees saw themselves as good examples because they thought they served God by insisting people achieve righteousness through specific rules and rituals.

But Jesus knew no one can work their way into God's righteousness. That's why he was down here, among the disreputable, including the disreputable Pharisees.

Our objective-in-Jesus is to make friends with others, including those who might be considered outsiders. And our message is this: "Become friends with God; he's already a friend with you" (2 Corinthians 5:20 MSG).

Just Be You

By the grace of God I am what I am,
and his grace to me was not without effect.
1 Corinthians 15:10

God wants you to be you.

You don't have to try to pretend to be someone else; you don't have to hide who you really are. The most attractive people I know are not the best looking; rather, they are authentic to who they are. There's no pretense about them.

You can relax knowing that being yourself is exactly what God wants of you. You bring glory to God just by being yourself because he created you to be just the person you are.

Now, *believe* you are who God says you are!

No one else has a vote on who you are. You are free to be you instead of imitating someone else. You are free to use your unique, God-given gifts, and there's no need to compare your gifts to the gifts of others.

No one else is in competition to be you!

Where are the places in your life where you are still trying to be someone else? Ask God to guide you to yourself.

NURTURING A QUIET SOUL

But I have stilled and quieted my soul; like a weaned child
with its mother, like a weaned child is my soul within me.
Psalm 131:2

My older sister, Lori Hensley, a serious prayer warrior, taught me to meditate on Psalm 131. The insights I gained helped me move toward God's peace that passes all understanding:

We keep our hearts humble. This doesn't mean we have a low opinion of ourselves. A humble heart means we know our position in Christ, and so we stop trying to be responsible for the things we were never responsible for. This frees us to live like God intended and allows us to make uncluttered choices that will move us closer to God.

We show the maturity of a weaned child. The nursing child demands immediate attention, but the weaned child trusts and is content to wait. We quietly center ourselves on God, peacefully, without agitation and anxiety, and trust God is actively supporting us.

We hope in the Lord with confident expectation. Truth says God will answer our prayers; he will respond to our needs and he will pave the path before us, now and forever (see also Psalm 18:36).

OBJECTIVE-IN-JESUS: RESPECT BY LISTENING

Be devoted to one another in brotherly love.
Honor one another above yourselves.
Romans 12:10

One of the simplest ways to show respect is to listen to the hidden hurts and heartaches, the deepest dreams and desires, of one another.

The truth is the God of the universe listens to our prayers. This does serious damage to any argument that we are too busy to listen — busier than God?

Jesus listened to those around him and he listens to us, which destroys the pretense that our mission is too important to take the time to listen. Or, is our mission, or even what we do day-to-day, more important than the mission Jesus was on?

Our objective-in-Jesus is to respect others enough to let them get the whole story out before we rush in to give an answer, or jump in to fix things, or just plain react to what we *think* instead of what is true.

You don't have to agree with what they say; that's another matter, but unless you hear them out, you won't even know what they mean. You show others respect, not because of who they are, but because of whom they belong to — the same One who created you.

Polar Bear Theology — Handling Temptation

Submit yourselves, then, to God.
Resist the devil, and he will flee from you.
James 4:7

When Leo Tolstoy was a boy, he reportedly started the "White Polar Bear Club" with two of his friends. In order to become a member, you had to stand in the corner and *not* think of a white polar bear for thirty consecutive minutes.

Have you ever tried to intentionally not think about something? The harder you try, the more impossible it becomes to keep out of your mind!

Yet, this is how we handle temptation; when it comes, we try as hard as we can to not think about what is tempting us. But the longer we think about not giving in, the more likely we will.

James says we should focus on God, not the temptation. When we focus on the Devil, we are focusing in the wrong direction.

I am not suggesting that we cannot say, "No, I'm not going to do that" to the enemy, just as Jesus said, "Get behind me, Satan!" What I am saying is that when we are tempted, we should turn toward God and away from the temptation. We resist the devil, by submitting to God.

SERVICE IS SACRIFICE

*This is how we know what love is: Jesus Christ laid down his
life for us. And we ought to lay down our lives for our brothers.*
1 John 3:16

Serving others comes at a sacrifice of time, money, energy,
even yourself: "I no longer live, but Christ lives in me" (Galatians 2:20).

Iron-man missionary Paul paid a heavy price for his service to others: "We serve God whether people honor us or
despise us, whether they slander us or praise us ... Our hearts
ache, but we always have joy. We are poor, but we give spiritual riches to others. We own nothing, and yet we have everything" (2 Corinthians 6:8, 10 NLT).

By serving others sacrificially, the apostle John says we
begin to grasp and experience godly love: "This is love: not
that we loved God, but that he loved us and sent his Son as an
atoning sacrifice for our sins. Dear friends, since God so loved
us, we also ought to love one another" (1 John 4:10–11).

Serve on God's terms, not at your own convenience. You
have been given the Spirit of Christ and he enables you to give
yourself sacrificially for others.

SET APART AND APPOINTED

Before you were born I set you apart
and appointed you as my spokesman to the world.
Jeremiah 1:5 (NLT, 1996 ed.)

Of all my teachers in school, the most influential was Judy Black, my English teacher at Miami Killian High School. Judy gave me the confidence that I was shaped to be a writer. She believed in me when not even I believed in myself. For years, when few people read what I wrote, she encouraged me.

In Jeremiah 1:5, we see that God created Jeremiah to share the Creator's message with the nations. I believe God shaped Judy Black to share her enthusiasm for English and literature with students like me. I now believe God shaped me to share my writing with others, and I believe God created you to share yourself with those around you.

When you hide yourself under a bushel, keeping your skills, talents, and insights hidden away from others, you not only diminish yourself; you also diminish the Christ-community that God intended for you to bless. God created you with a uniqueness that enriches the world when you give yourself to the community around you.

Ask God to show you how to use your skills, talents, and insights in service to those around you.

Since I Was a Child

"All these I have kept since I was a boy," he said.
Luke 18:21

Here is a man who loves God and has worked hard to keep all the commandments since he was a boy. Yet, he is still uncertain about his status in heaven and his place within the family of God. So he goes to Jesus, asking what else he must do to earn his way into heaven.

Jesus says, "You still lack one thing . . ." (Luke 18:22). But in this, he challenges the young man to give up childish thinking. In a sense, Jesus says, "You have been keeping the commandments since you were a boy. But now it is time to mature."

Paul later explained what such maturity is: "You are grown sons, and the Father will soon send the Holy Spirit into your hearts, allowing you to have an intimate, direct relationship with God. He will tell you what to do, as if the commandments were written into your heart" (Galatians 4:1–7, author paraphrase).

We inherit eternal life, not by doing something but by belonging to someone — by being children of the Father, joint-heirs with Jesus, accepted in the family of God.

STAINED GLASS SAINTS

*It is God himself who has made us what we are
and given us new lives from Christ Jesus.*
Ephesians 2:10 (LB)

God loves variety and created each of us with different shapes, interests, and personalities; yet, just as all humans have foundational features, such as a common blood system, we all reflect the same Creator.

To see it another way, we are like stained glass and our different personalities reflect God's light in a variety of colors and patterns.

Each of us is a unique, one-of-a-kind, never-to-be-repeated expression of Christ. Steve Pettit says, "There is a sacramental nature to our particular personalities and, within the family, the God-given freedom to be who we were created to be."

Our uniqueness comes with a God-given responsibility to look out for one another in love, to know and to be known, to love and to be loved, and to encourage each other to reach the fullest expression of Christ-in-me that we can be.

Our objective-in-Jesus is to help each other become the best picture of Jesus we can be.

ON PURPOSE WITH PEOPLE

*"Does he not leave the ninety-nine in the open country
and go after the lost sheep until he finds it?"*
Luke 15:4

We never see Jesus rushing. He always takes time for people; he stops and he listens. He even sought the one while the ninety-nine waited.

Jesus kept a steady, unrushed pace because he stayed connected to his unrushed Father. He could have filled every minute of a day timer with things to do, but the first thing he always did was go to the Father.

Despite the enormity of his purpose and the value of his time, Jesus spent time with the Father. Does Jesus know something we don't know, or do we just think we have more important things to do than to maintain an intimate relationship with the Father, as Jesus did?

It's safe to say that our purpose will involve relationships with the people around us and that God placed them in our lives so we could pour *our lives* into them. Our purpose begins with the relationship we have with an unrushed Savior, who steadies us as we invest in people, not things, moving with a rhythm of grace that beats like the heart of the Father.

Our objective-in-Jesus is to take time for Jesus and then, following his priorities, take time for others.

THE GOD OF HOPE

*And hope does not disappoint us, because God has
poured out his love into our hearts by the Holy Spirit.*
Romans 5:5

A few years ago I became extremely ill and, for about six months, I was unable to walk any farther than the mailbox. Needless to say, I gained weight and found myself facing a huge challenge. I needed to lose more pounds than there are days in a month!

I found myself feeling hopeless — the kind of hopelessness that makes you think, "What's the use? I might as well not even try."

No doubt you can relate, not necessarily about the weight, but about the feeling of hopelessness. Maybe you are in a marriage or facing health issues and you find yourself thinking, "What's the use?" Or perhaps you are in a frustrating job, facing a difficult family issue, or dealing with the death of the most important person in your life.

We serve a God of hope (Romans 5:5), and his is a hope that will not disappoint. This hope we have is based in a relationship with the One who provides hope when everything seems hopeless; who fills us with hope when there is nothing left except for him, our Father, Almighty God. We can trust him to help us grow as we persevere by his strength, and even overcome difficult situations.

THE MAKE-IT-OBVIOUS PRAYER

*"We are bringing you good news, telling you to turn
from these worthless things to the living God, who made
heaven and earth and sea and everything in them."*
Acts 14:15

One time God pressed on my heart that I should tell a fellow writer the good news about Jesus. I wasn't sure about the best way to bring up the subject, so I asked God to open the door in a way that was obvious.

The next day the writer came in and started telling me about an idea for a story. He said, "What if God couldn't get people to listen to him, and so he came to earth looking like an average guy, sitting in a bar, telling all these people getting drunk that life had more meaning."

The Holy Spirit nudged me as if to say, "Is that obvious enough?"

Sometimes we need to pray the make-it-obvious prayer and ask God to give us opportunities to tell others about Jesus. Pray that God will prepare the hearts of those you'll be speaking to, and pray for God to soften your heart, then watch how he gives you a burden for the lost.

THE MASTER'S
INSTRUCTIONAL DESIGN

"The Holy Spirit ... will teach you all things."
John 14:26

I am told that once you get into medical school you are no longer given specific A – B – C grades. Instead, your progress is measured by a pass/fail standard: Did you master the training or did you fail to master the training?

God works on such a mastery-based system. His commitment to us is greater than letting us settle for a D in "love thy neighbor." He wants us to get it right, but knows we can't the first time or every time, so he keeps working with us until we get it. A failed test just means we train again until we can pass the test. In failing, there is no disgrace, only his grace.

Our Teacher makes use of all things—pain and suffering, joy and comfort, opposition and cooperation—to transform us into a people who love fully and deeply, who become other-centered instead of self-centered.

God will continue to work with you until you are successful at the purpose for which he created you, and then he will welcome you home when you graduate to heaven (Romans 8:28; Philippians 3:14).

JESUS IN ME SETS ME FREE

"Then you will know the truth, and the truth will set you free."
John 8:32

Jesus, you are the Truth and the Truth sets me free. You are the Truth and your truth lives in me.

I clothe myself in your truth, Jesus, putting on the coat of a new self, "created to be like God in true righteousness and holiness" (Ephesians 4:24). You are "the way and the truth and the life" and I am connected to God through you and you alone (John 14:6). Because of you, I know the truth about who I am and I know that your life is working in me (Galatians 2:20).

Your truth enables me to discern and reject the lies of the enemy. Your truth demolishes arguments and pretensions that are at war with the knowledge of God. In your truth, I will "take captive every thought" and make it obedient to you (2 Corinthians 10:5).

I can trust your leadership, I can trust your commands, and I can trust your plans because you are the Truth.

TO THINK AS JESUS THINKS

But we understand these things,
for we have the mind of Christ.
1 Corinthians 2:16 (NLT)

The apostle Paul tells us we have the "mind of Christ," and that means we have the capacity to think as Jesus thinks. But our response to Paul is more often "Yeah, right!" than "Yeah God!" We just hope we can manage this Jesus-life without majorly embarrassing ourselves.

I mean, who can know the mind of God? Maybe the saints, maybe the pros? Even the Hall of Fame prophet Isaiah asked a similar question: "Is there anyone around who knows God's Spirit, anyone who knows what he is doing?" (1 Corinthians 2:16 MSG).

But then Paul, the teacher's pet, the guy who is always raising his hand in class when the rest of us are ducking down to avoid being called on — you know, *that* Paul — he answers Isaiah's probing question so simply it can scarcely be believed.

Teacher: "Does anyone know what God is doing, or even thinking? Yes, Paul, I see your hand. What do you think the answer is?"

"Christ knows," says Paul, "and we have Christ's Spirit" (1 Corinthians 2:16 MSG).

THEN, I HOPE YOU NEVER SIN

"You wicked servant ... I canceled all that debt of yours because you begged me to. Shouldn't you have had mercy on your fellow servant just as I had on you?"
Matthew 18:32–33

Jesus told a story about a servant, deeply in debt to the king, who pleaded for mercy. The king canceled his entire debt.

Almost immediately after leaving the king's presence, the servant saw someone who owed him money. The debt was just a fraction of what the servant had owed to the king, yet the servant had this man thrown into debtor's prison!

When the king heard what happened, he ordered the forgiven, yet merciless servant brought back before him. Outraged, the king said, "Shouldn't you have had mercy on your fellow servant just as I had on you?" He then ordered the unforgiving servant to debtor's prison until he'd paid back every penny of his debt.

Jesus finished by saying, "That's what my heavenly Father will do to you if you refuse to forgive your brothers and sisters in your heart."

John Wesley said: "If you are unwilling to forgive, then I hope you never sin."

Truth: God Loves through Me

Love does no harm to its neighbor.
Therefore love is the fulfillment of the law.
Romans 13:10

In faith, I know this to be true:

I can love others as much as God loves me because God loves through me. God's love in me allows me to love others with the same love God has for them (John 13:34–36; 15:12). In faith, I believe this to be true and so I choose to love like it is true.

By God's grace, I am resolved to love others with whatever means God gives me. I can do this because he commands, "Love your neighbor as yourself," and he would not give me a command without giving me the ability to follow it (Matthew 22:39).

I have the means to love others because it is part of a royal decree passed to me from the King of kings (James 2:8).

I have the means to love others because I am a fully privileged member of God's family, and he has given me the authority to share his love with others (Romans 12:10).

By loving others, I engage the power of God's mercy and grace as love becomes "the fulfillment of the law" (Romans 13:10).

TRUTH: I AM ABLE TO LOVE

"But love your enemies, do good to them, and lend to them without expecting to get anything back."
Luke 6:35

In faith, I know this to be true:

By God's grace, I am able to love with abandonment. This other-centered love is unconditional; it makes no attempt to force people to do things and no attempt to control them (Romans 12:19). I love with godly love when I give expecting nothing in return (Luke 6:35).

By God's grace, my love is filled with patience, kindness, encouragement, humility, service, trust, truth, hope, perseverance, and joy, and I cover the wrongs of those I love (1 Corinthians 13:1 – 13).

By God's grace, my love is sincere, serves with zeal, and is Spirit-directed. My love is faithful in prayer, generous in invitation, and full of blessings for those who oppose me.

I cry with others, I laugh with others, and I live in harmony as best I can, while loving from the center of God's love (Romans 12:9 – 21).

In faith, I believe God's love is more powerful than any force in all eternity (1 Corinthians 13:13), and I live according to that truth.

Until We Are Fully Known

*Now I know in part; then I shall know fully,
even as I am fully known.*
1 Corinthians 13:12

The failure to communicate in a relationship can be extremely frustrating. But, the failure to commune leads us to despair.

Communication is mostly about sharing information; communion is about sharing life. In communion, we know others and others know us. We care for others and they care for us on a deep and intimate level.

One of the deepest needs we have as humans is to know that we are fully known, including our deepest, darkest secrets, and, yet, still be deeply loved. We need to know that despite our failures and weaknesses, regardless of our successes and strengths, we are still unconditionally loved.

The truth is we are fully known and loved by God. He draws us to himself, where we come face-to-face with his perfect love.

Our objective-in-Jesus is to carry this "fully known," perfect love to the lives of others, modeling Christlike communion, where it is safe to be completely transparent with others and still be unconditionally loved.

TRUTH: WEEDING OUT WHAT DOESN'T BELONG

"Like a scarecrow in a melon patch, their idols cannot speak;
they must be carried because they cannot walk. Do not fear
them; they can do no harm nor can they do any good."
Jeremiah 10:5

In faith, I know this to be true:

By God's grace, I am able to take control of my thoughts, weeding out the ones that don't belong — those that might lead me away from God.

This is a choice I make; I am not helpless in controlling my mind. God has already given me powerful tools "for smashing warped philosophies, tearing down barriers erected against the truth of God, fitting every loose thought and emotion and impulse into the structure of life shaped by Christ" (2 Corinthians 10:5 MSG). These God-given tools are ready for me to use and they clear the ground for my growth toward maturity (2 Corinthians 10:6 MSG).

It is true that I am more than a conqueror through God, who loves me (Romans 8:37). God renews my spirit and calls me to a single-minded purpose, aligned with his heart and mind (Psalm 51:10; James 1:5 – 8; 4:8).

WANTED: SLAVE FOR
SACRIFICIAL SERVICE

*"Will he not first sit down and estimate the cost
to see if he has enough money to complete it?"*
Luke 14:28

Not too many of us would be attracted to a career as a slave; yet, that's exactly what God is raising us to be — sacrificial servants, motivated by the nature of God working within us.

Sacrificial love destroys our comfort zones because it requires we lay down our demands that life be lived on our terms. It's a radical shift from what we often do — serving others as long as our interests and preferences are protected, as long as we get credit for what we have done.

In sacrificial relationships, someone pays the price so others can freely receive. All we have from God is freely received, paid for through the passionate sacrifice of Jesus Christ (1 Corinthians 4:7). And, now, we sacrificially give to others.

Our objective-in-Jesus is to count the cost of godly love, but then, regardless of how much sacrifice it requires, we pay the price so others can experience firsthand the sacrificial nature of God's love.

By God's grace, our witness becomes so rare that the world takes notice of such sacrificial service.

WE BEGIN AGAIN WITH NIGHT

"But even if he does not, we want you to know,
O king, that we will not serve your gods."
Daniel 3:18

In his book *Night*, Elie Wiesel describes the unholy madness he faced during World War II as a prisoner in the deadly German concentration camps of Auschwitz and Buchenwald.

Before he was sixteen, Wiesel witnessed the death of his father, presumed his mother and sister were dead, and felt as if everything had come to an end, including his faith in God.

Wiesel, an orthodox Jew, records with honesty his anger at God for appearing to ignore those who cried out for the Almighty's protection. And who can judge a crumbling faith under such circumstances, particularly when we know our faith often crumbles under far less?

Perhaps the most difficult lesson in the school of Christ is facing the fire and wondering if God is still on his throne. Like Shadrach, Meshach, and Abednego, our objective-in-Jesus is to grow in confidence that the God we serve is able to save us and, if he doesn't, we can still be certain his plans for us are not evil but are to give us an eternal future and hope (Jeremiah 29:11).

We Do from the Life Within

Don't become so well-adjusted to your culture that you fit into it without even thinking. Instead, fix your attention on God. You'll be changed from the inside out.
Romans 12:2 (MSG)

On a warm and windy day in downtown Nashville, my friend Doug held the door to a building open for a woman coming in just behind him.

She said, "You don't have to hold the door open for me just because I'm a woman."

He smiled, saying, "I'm not holding the door open for you because you're a woman; I'm holding it open for you because I'm a gentleman."

Regardless of what you may think of disappearing, old school courtesy, the point I want to make is this: we do things because of who we are in Christ, not because of who someone else is in life.

We open doors, if you will, because we are one with Jesus, not because of who someone else is or who someone expects us to be or who the culture thinks we ought to be.

And when we open doors, we say, "I do this because I am a Jesus-one. I do this because Jesus is present in me."

WHERE YOUR HOPES ARE HUNG

But hope that is seen is no hope at all.
Who hopes for what he already has?
Romans 8:24

Our faith is hammered out in the everyday, mundane experiences of our lives. The things we truly believe emerge in these interactions and make us see with painful clarity where we have been hanging our hope, such as on a paycheck, a circumstance, a job, or a relationship.

Can you see that when we place more hope in those things than we do in Jesus, he is compelled to pull their hooks off the wall, pushing us to pick up our hopes and hang them on the one who hung on the cross for us? When we avoid difficult life experiences, we also avoid the very path that will lead us to an intimate and mature relationship with Jesus.

Consider this question: If you could believe your current circumstances or problems are part of God's redemptive plan to bring you closer to him, how would you behave differently?

Before you answer, read the story of Joseph in Genesis.

Clearing Obstacles to Unity

*"Therefore, if you are offering your gift at the altar and there
remember that your brother has something against you ...
first go and be reconciled to your brother."*
Matthew 5:23–24

Imagine looking out your window and seeing your neighbor back his car into yours, leaving a sizeable dent. He sees you watching but drives away.

You see each other in the neighborhood and at church, but he never mentions the incident. For weeks you carry on an internal debate about confronting him. Finally, as he's getting into his *dent-free* car, you approach him and say, "You hit my car last month."

"Yes, I did."

"Why haven't you talked to me?"

"Because I talked to God about it," he says. "I confessed what I did at the altar and even gave extra offering to pay for it. So, God has forgiven me and everything is okay."

Sound crazy? When Jesus says reconcile with your brother before worshiping, he is pointing toward a similar scenario.

God forgives us of our sins, but before we praise him, we are to remove obstacles such as guilt, unresolved conflict, or bitter attitudes. Jesus emphasizes relationships over rituals, people over process. Our objective-in-Jesus is to remove anything that keeps us from oneness with God and unity with Jesus-ones.

FAITH-FILLED RISKS

*He replied, "I tell you that to everyone who has,
more will be given, but as for the one who has nothing,
even what he has will be taken away."*
Luke 19:26

Jesus once told the story of a master who asked three servants to handle his money while he was away. When he returned, the first servant had doubled the master's money, and the second had earned a 50 percent return.

But the third servant, in essence, said he had been afraid the master would punish him for making a mistake, so he hid the money in the cellar until the master returned.

The master rewarded the first two servants, saying those who handle small matters well will be given greater responsibility. But he rebuked the third servant for *faithlessly* playing it safe.

Our faith in Jesus grows when we take risks—not just any kind of risks, but ones that are specifically directed by God. These God-nudges push us beyond the borders of our "independent states" into the "promised land" of life by faith.

Our objective-in-Jesus is to mature in the truth that any decision made independently of God is a faithless decision. Make mistakes, but live in faith.

Representing God's Gold Medal

... as though God were making his appeal through us.
2 Corinthians 5:20

During the 2008 Olympics in Beijing, Swedish wrestler Ara Abrahamian, angry that he didn't win the gold medal, threw down his bronze medal during the awards ceremony and stormed off into infamy.

He not only violated the Olympic spirit, but did so without any regard to the fact that he was representing his country, all the people of Sweden.

My imagination meandered to a fictional interview with Abrahamian, where he might have said, "I'm here to represent my country and I wanted people to know Sweden is more than blond babes, Abba, Volvo, and IKEA."

Back in reality, we are told by Paul, a gold medalist in following Christ, that we are to represent Jesus in our Olympic walk with God. It should be as if "God were making his appeal through us" (2 Corinthians 5:20).

Now before you start thinking "I ought" and "I must," remember you have already determined "you can't," but "God can." Instead of focusing on how you have to *act* to represent Jesus, focus on the truth that the Holy Spirit is at work inside you and his work will transform you into the very image of Christ.

Sorting Coins

Therefore no one will be declared righteous in his sight
by observing the law; rather, through the law
we become conscious of sin.
Romans 3:20

Recently, I went to a coin-sorting machine and poured in a huge bag of change. The total came to $22.31. I took the receipt to customer service and the cashier gave me 22 dollars in bills and 31 cents. I still had change.

I could have counted out the exact amount of change to total an even dollar amount, like $22.00 and *no* cents, and poured that into the coin-sorting machine. But then I would have been counting the change myself, and I would not have needed to use the machine. Argh!

When we try to live by the law, it's like we are pouring change into a coin-sorting machine, always hoping to get an even dollar amount.

The frustration we feel when we stumble and fail is absolutely normal. In truth, it is part of God's plan. By realizing how far we fall short, we come to the place of "I can't, but God can." And it is there that we are able to live in the unhurried movement of God's grace.

FEARING FRIENDSHIP

"Everyone who does evil hates the light, and will not come
into the light for fear that his deeds will be exposed."
John 3:20

Although you and I share the same Holy Spirit within, we may have difficulty developing a deep, transparent friendship together. My fear is that, in order to truly know other people, I must allow them to get close enough to see the real me. What if there are parts of me that I am not proud of, or that need a lot of work? Never fear! Truth is here.

Jesus invites you to know him, so you can get used to being in a transparent, authentic relationship. Jesus went to the cross and beyond to guarantee you would be accepted into God's family through your intimate relationship with him (Ephesians 1:6–7).

You now live by the Truth, so you can stay in the light, letting people plainly see what God is doing in your life. This includes how far he has brought you from your past and how he is still working with you, despite your failures and fears.

Your intimate friendship with Jesus will help you enter into deep, authentic relationships with others, where you know them and you are known by them.

OUR MIGHTY FORTRESS

The LORD Almighty is with us; the God of Jacob is our fortress.
Psalm 46:11

Many of us are familiar with this psalm because of Martin Luther's majestic hymn, "A Mighty Fortress Is Our God." The psalm reminds us that God is our mighty fortress; he is "our refuge and strength, an ever-present help in trouble" (Psalm 46:1). Luther wrote this:

> *Did we in our own strength confide,*
> *Our striving would be losing;*
> *Were not the right Man on our side,*
> *The Man of God's own choosing.*
> *Dost ask who that may be? Christ Jesus, it is He;*
> *Lord Sabaoth His Name,*
> *From age to age the same,*
> *And He must win the battle.*

The thing is this—God is not just beside us; he himself is our strength and that allows us, in faith, to make a choice not to be afraid, even when our lives are in turmoil.

Our objective-in-Jesus is to grow confident in the truth that even when we face chaos and uncertainty, even if the mountains tumble into the seas and the waters threaten to drown us; God is with us, working inside, outside, and all around us (Psalm 46:2–3, 11).

FORGIVING YOURSELF

Then he said to him, "Follow me!"
John 21:19

We believe God will forgive us; the problem, though, is we won't forgive ourselves.

Peter knew the feeling. He had failed Jesus, so he went back to fishing. He had set a high standard of loyalty and love to his Lord, only to fail — not once, not twice, but three times. How could Jesus forgive him when he couldn't even forgive himself?

But then Jesus, resurrected, yelled, "Ahoy!" from the shore. They ate breakfast and Peter probably hung back feeling he wasn't worthy to even be in the presence of Jesus.

Yet, Jesus, showing sweet sensitivity, reached out to Peter. Knowing he was hurting and humiliated, but also knowing he had been humbled into the place of "I can't," he reminded Peter that the sentence does not stop at "I can't." It moves on to "God can."

Our objective-in-Jesus is to develop a confidence in the truth that God forgives us, so it's okay to forgive ourselves.

LASER SURGERY

For the word of God is living and active.
Sharper than any double-edged sword, it penetrates even to
dividing soul and spirit, joints and marrow; it judges
the thoughts and attitudes of the heart.
Hebrews 4:12

A few years ago, a cyst developed under the skin on the palm of my right hand that made typing difficult. The surgery I faced was delicate, requiring the surgeon to cut at just the right point so the entire cyst would be removed without damaging the mechanics of my hand. The surgeon was confident he could do this, but because it dealt with my writing hand, I was nervous about going under the knife.

As it turned out, the surgeon did an excellent job; my fingers work fine as I type this sentence.

I say this to illustrate the point that God's Word is as delicate and precise as a surgeon skillfully removing a cyst from cartilage. The Great Physician operates with perfection as he slices away our bad attitudes, thoughts, motives, and actions, "laying us open to listen and obey" (Hebrews 4:13 MSG).

Our objective-in-Jesus is this: we no longer fear the surgery because our faith is in the Almighty Surgeon.

CHEERFUL GENEROSITY

*Each man should give what he has decided in his heart
to give, not reluctantly or under compulsion,
for God loves a cheerful giver.*
2 Corinthians 9:7

When Paul says God loves a cheerful giver, he means God loves us to give cheerfully in all we do, not just when giving money. We need to apply more creativity to our generosity.

To help you think outside the box, start by asking these questions:

What talents and abilities do I have that can be shared with others in the name of Jesus?

What do I have in excess that, perhaps, God means for me to give or share with someone else?

Then, brainstorm how you can use what you have:

Can you cook? Consider preparing meals for people in your neighborhood or teach other people to cook. Do you have perfectly good items lying around that you hardly ever use? Give them to someone in need.

Our objective-in-Jesus is to share our time, talents, gifts, and blessings with others generously and creatively.

IS LIFE TOGETHER TOO HARD?

*Let us therefore make every effort to do what leads
to peace and to mutual edification.*
Romans 14:19

Some days I look into the faces of my two boys and see
sweet angels; other days I want to yell, "Can't you two just
get along?" I wonder if God looks at us — the community of
believers — and sighs, "Can't you children just get along?"

There are hundreds of reasons we don't get along, with
the sin of pride right at the top of the list. But I think one
huge reason we fail to live in authentic, consistent, committed
Christian community is because *it's too hard*.

Remaining transparent and honest and paying close
attention to the needs and concerns of one another requires
time-consuming effort. Frankly, it's easier to stay superficial
than it is to dig deeper into relationships that require patience
when we misunderstand, and "stick with it" stamina when we
see conflict coming.

Yet, if we will do the "hard work of getting along," we
can develop a "healthy, robust community that lives right
with God," one where we "one anothers" live in peace and joy
with each other (see James 3:18 MSG).

THE ARMOR OF GOD

Stand firm then, with the belt of truth . . .
the breastplate of righteousness . . . take up the shield of faith,
with which you can extinguish all the flaming arrows
of the evil one. Take the helmet of salvation and the sword
of the Spirit, which is the word of God.
Ephesians 6:14 – 17

God has provided you with the tools to stand your ground on the front lines of spiritual warfare. Pray: "Father, in Jesus' name, I put on the belt of truth that helps me know that the one who is in me is greater than the one who is in the world (1 John 4:4).

"Today I put on the breastplate of righteousness to respond from truth and not emotions, and strap on the sandals of the gospel of peace to help others make peace with you.

"Thank you for the protection that comes from the shield of faith, the helmet of salvation, and the sword of the Spirit, which is your Word.

"Lord, I set my mind and heart on you today, dedicating this whole day to you. I only want your will for my life. Through the name and blood of Jesus, amen."

Resembling
the Prodigal's Father

"But the father said to his servants,
'Quick! Bring the best robe and put it on him.
Put a ring on his finger and sandals on his feet.'"
Luke 15:22

In the story of the prodigal, we identify with the younger brother, seeing ourselves as prodigals returning to God.

Some of us even identify with the older brother, realizing we've sinfully harbored resentment when God shows grace to others who, in our wrongful judgment, are less Christian than ourselves.

But Henri Nouwen asks the provocative question: Have you ever thought God wants you to identify with the prodigal's father, who "keeps no record of wrongs" as he scans the horizon always hoping for the return of his son (1 Corinthians 13:5)?

Consider that we are on a journey, through Jesus, to become like the heavenly Father — one with his heart, one with his mind, and one with his other-centered focus. When we resemble Jesus, we resemble the Father (John 10:30).

To echo Oswald Chambers, "Do you not want to be a saint, or do you not believe God can make you one?"

The Things
That You Have Heard

*Let the word of Christ dwell in you richly as you teach
and admonish one another with all wisdom.*
Colossians 3:16

God wants you to teach someone who can then teach
someone else.

- He wants you to teach others about the spiritual
  insights he has deposited in you.
- He wants you to teach others about the ways he has
  stretched your faith.
- He wants you to teach others how they can discover life
  in Christ.

You may be wondering if you are capable of doing this,
but the apostle Paul says you can make a choice to "let the
message about Christ, in all its richness, fill your lives. Teach
and counsel each other with all the wisdom he gives" (Colossians 3:16 NLT).

Trust the indwelling of the Holy Spirit to flow from you
and give you the words and the wisdom you need to pass on
what God has taught you.

DOING OUTREACH SIDE-BY-SIDE

Whether I come and see you or only hear about you
in my absence, I will know that you stand firm in one spirit,
contending as one man for the faith of the gospel.
Philippians 1:27

Instead of seeing evangelism as something you have to do on your own, work together with some other believers. In a group, you'll find God is telling each of you to pray for, encourage, or support someone with Jesus-love. Write down all the names and as a group, pray for them in these four ways:

- *Pray for an opportunity to talk about Jesus* (Colossians 4:3). God will take you seriously and answer your prayer.
- *Pray for God to prepare hearts* (Acts 16:14). Anytime you see someone going through a storm in life, you can know that God is softening a heart.
- *Pray for God to tenderize your heart.* Ask God to make your heart tender toward a specific person or group of people.
- *Pray that the words of Jesus "will simply take off* and race through the country to a ground-swell of response" (2 Thessalonians 3:1 MSG), just as they did among the early Christians.

THE MIND OF
MERE HUMAN BEINGS

*Jesus turned and said to Peter, "Get behind me, Satan!
You are a stumbling block to me; you do not have in mind
the things of God, but the things of men."*
Matthew 16:23

Insecurity demands that I must always be in control, must always have the last word, and must always have my way.

Insecurity leads to power struggles, and the result is that we live in perpetual conflict. When pressed, we can even try to snatch something out of God's hands, the way a child will grab something from another.

In a sense, Peter is doing just that. When Jesus explains God's plan, Peter tries to snatch it from the Lord's hands: "Never, Lord!" he says. "This shall never happen to you!" Jesus rebukes Peter for "seeing things merely from a human point of view, not from God's" (Matthew 16:23 NLT).

When we think like mere human beings, we distract ourselves from God's plan and we get in the way of God's purpose. Jesus' rebuke isn't a final statement of our dim-witted humanity; rather, it's an exhortation than we can match our minds with God as we let the mind of Christ carry us to the things above.

OBJECTIVE-IN-JESUS: GOD'S VIEW

Not many of you were wise by human standards; not many were influential; not many were of noble birth.

1 Corinthians 1:26

Jesus regarded everyone he met from an other-world perspective, seeing them as eternal beings, refusing to let their circumstances or sins define who they were.

This perspective, so different from our own, brought out the best in the people Jesus met. He saw their true value, and as a result, they came to know their true value.

Consider what Jesus saw:

- A man who was able to see when others saw a blind man.
- A man walking when others saw a cripple.
- An articulate disciple when others saw a tax collector named Matthew.
- Men who did not know what they were doing when others saw nameless soldiers pounding nails into a cross.

Our objective-in-Jesus is to stop seeing others from our limited perspective and to start seeing them the way God sees them. We should be encouraging them so that their best emerges, and we should be bringing them to the one who wants what is best for all people in the world (Luke 2:8 – 10).

WE ARE FAM − I − LY

Now you can call God your dear Father.
Now you are no longer a slave but God's own child.
And since you are his child, everything he has belongs to you.
Galatians 4:6−7 (NLT, 1996 ed.)

We are a family forged by the fires of God's love. Yet, for many of us, this image fails because we have only seen broken models, shattered relationships, and hurting hearts. The good news is that God will provide you with the very things you have longed for in a family through a community committed to Christ.

In small groups of believers we belong and we help others belong. We learn that it takes honesty, vulnerability, effort, and a lot of forgiveness to make relationships work. We *unlearn* the unhealthy methods of relating to one another that we learned living in families fallen and fearful, or the survival mechanisms we adopted maneuvering through the playground or the cafeteria at school.

Since you are part of this God-family, you now have a chance to start fresh in developing healthy relationships, godly character, and biblical values.

WORKMANSHIP

*For we are God's workmanship, created in Christ Jesus to do
good works, which God prepared in advance for us to do.*
Ephesians 2:10

When it comes to being creatures of our Creator, we
often think of God being far away building babies through
mass production.

The Bible says that is not the way it works. God designed
each of us individually and specifically and spoke us into
our mothers' wombs, no different than the way he spoke the
world into existence.

We need to abandon any thoughts of creation being mass
produced. Let us start thinking of God as a master artist at
work, like Rembrandt or Michelangelo, who may have spent
weeks working on the corner of a canvas in order to get just
the right shading and shadow.

God thought about you. He gave you just the right eye
color and smile. You are God's masterpiece and he carefully,
lovingly selected everything else that makes you YOU.

If you have been rejecting God's design of you, talk to
him about your frustrations, disappointments, or confusion.
When you are ready, thank God for how he designed you.

Holy Spirit Timing

*Trust in the LORD with all your heart and lean not
on your own understanding; in all your ways acknowledge him,
and he will make your paths straight.*
Proverbs 3:5–6

When I was in college, I planned to buy a computer through a program offered by the university. But when I turned in my paperwork, they told me the program had been discontinued for a few months. I remember being so angry at God.

Perhaps you've prayed in a similar fashion: "God, you know I need this (insert your own item). What do I do now?"

About two months later, the university started selling the computers through a new program that offered an upgraded model, this time bundled with free software that they had previously charged for. The whole package was cheaper than the original offer. Can you say, "Spiritual egg on my face"?

We have this Spirit inside us, and God wants us to listen and discern through the Holy Spirit because the Spirit connects us to God. The Holy Spirit does not speak on his own; he speaks only what he hears from God.

THE TIME CAME

While they were there, the time came for the baby to be born.
Luke 2:6

We manage time; we waste time. We spend time; we save time. We wish the time would come; we wish the time would pass. We see time fly; we feel time drag. We watch clocks and carry calendars, creating the illusion that we somehow control time, yet God controls time.

He created time and we, his creations, are fenced by his time, directed and guided by his holy and loving hand. Do you think God was surprised that "while they were there, the time came for her baby to be born"?

We are often surprised by unexpected developments in our lives; yet the Bible teaches that God is never surprised. God is working to bring you into eternity, not just to *get you through the end of next week*. Praise God for his grace and for a love so strong that he wants you to spend an eternity with him.

If you were to believe that God is not surprised by your current circumstances and that, at this very moment, he is working out a holy and healthy resolution for you, how would you live differently?

LOVE GOD WITH
YOUR WHOLE HEART

"Love the Lord your God with all your heart and with all your soul and with all your strength and with all your mind."
Luke 10:27

In order to love God with all your strength, you have to admit you are weak. By doing this, you acknowledge God is the true source of your strength and that in your weakness he is strong. You become strong as you become totally dependent upon him, allowing his strength to work through you (2 Corinthians 12:9–10).

As God shows his strength through you, you will find yourself doing things you never thought possible. God promises you can do all things through him as he gives you *his strength* (Philippians 4:13). You will take steps of faith you never thought possible, and you will love others in a way you never imagined as God supplies you with supernatural strength and energy.

Tell God you need his strength and really mean it this time. When you try to love and serve others with just your strength, you will inevitably fail. And that's okay, because God wants you to fail in your own strength so that you will start relying upon his strength. Tell God you need his strength, but, this time, really mean it.

NEGOTIATING FORGIVENESS

"For if you forgive men when they sin against you,
your heavenly Father will also forgive you. But if you do not
forgive men their sins, your Father will not forgive your sins."
Matthew 6:14–15

When it comes to forgiveness, we are tough negotiators. We open with an offer like, "I'll forgive you, if ..." Then, we follow with a subtle concession: "I can't forgive her until she learns her lesson." Finally, we take off the gloves: "If I forgive him, he'll just think he got away with it."

We think we're negotiating for God; we think we're negotiating for justice, when all we are really doing is negotiating for control over the situation.

But God's instructions are clear and unambiguous: If you forgive those who sin against you, then God will forgive you for your sins against him. If you do not forgive those who sin against you, then God will not forgive you for your sins against him. No room for negotiation there.

The question is not, *should, if, or can* someone be forgiven; the true question is, will you make the choice to forgive?

TRUTH: GOD MANAGES CIRCUMSTANCES

Whether you turn to the right or to the left, your ears will hear a voice behind you, saying, "This is the way; walk in it."
Isaiah 30:21

In faith, I know this to be true: God manages circumstances.

He makes my paths straight as I lean on him and acknowledge him (Proverbs 3:5–6). He has placed a hedge around me and he blesses the work of my hands (Job 1:10).

God says he is the only one capable of interpreting circumstances: "For my thoughts are not your thoughts, neither are your ways my ways" (Isaiah 55:8).

When I begin to see circumstances as God sees them, I "will go out in joy and be led forth in peace; the mountains and hills will burst into song before [me], and all the trees of the field will clap their hands" (Isaiah 55:12).

Praise God! He sees the path before us and calls us forth in faith (Genesis 22:12), showing us there are no coincidences in this universe of his design.

DON'T WASTE THE GRACE

*As God's fellow workers we urge you not to receive
God's grace in vain.*
2 Corinthians 6:1

There are days I want to pack it all in and quit this Jesus-*thing*. In some ways life was much easier before the Holy Spirit began his work in me. Back then, I could simply lie to get out of a difficult situation; I could pretend my little world was *the world*.

The problem is, it's not a Jesus-thing, it's a Jesus-*life*, and quitting is not an option. He who began this good work in me is not going to bail on me, ever.

God gives us grace sufficient for our needs each day, every day. In 2 Corinthians 6:1, Paul, in effect, says, don't waste God's grace; don't receive God's grace in vain, rejecting it in order to nurture frustrations and disappointments.

In other words, God's power—the very strength we need, the very testimony we were meant to model—emerges in troubles, hardships, and distresses (2 Corinthians 6:4). Our objective-in-Jesus is to stay at our posts in these uncertain times and not waste the grace God has given us.

PROMETHEAN GRATITUDE

*I long, yes, I faint with longing to enter the courts of the LORD.
With my whole being, body and soul, I will shout
joyfully to the living God.*
Psalm 84:2 (NLT)

In Greek mythology, Prometheus stole fire from Zeus and gave it to the human race. We too steal things from the One True God:

- *We steal* when we take matters into our own hands, thinking God is too slow or not coming at all.
- *We steal* when we insist on our own answer instead of being content with God's.
- *We steal* when we grab for something we want, because we think God won't give it to us.
- *We steal* when we take credit for something that only happened because God worked through us.

The problem with this Promethean pattern is that it destroys our ability to be grateful. We begin to think that if we take something, we have gotten it ourselves, no thanks to God or anyone else.

Gratitude is one gauge that measures our dependency on God. The more dependent we are, the more grateful we become.

RE-CREATING A PURE HEART

Create in me a pure heart, O God,
and renew a steadfast spirit within me.
Psalm 51:10

O God, create in me a pure heart:

- A heart that won't run with lust after physical pleasure.
- A heart that obediently refuses what you have fenced away as sin.
- A heart that argues for love instead of fairness.

O God, create in me a pure heart:

- A heart that never boasts about what it has or what it has done.
- A heart that walks humbly, not trying to appear more important than it is.
- A heart of love that never insists on its own way.

O God, create in me a pure heart:

- A heart that looks to you for provision.
- A heart that looks on the things above and not the things below.
- A heart that chases furiously after you.

Father, renew a steadfast spirit within me:

- A spirit not double-minded, but focused uncompromisingly on your purpose.
- A spirit resolved to know Christ and Christ alone.
- My God, please make this so.

BLIND TRUTH: REFUSING TO SEE

*The Jews still did not believe that he had been blind and had
received his sight until they sent for the man's parents.*
John 9:18

When Jesus healed the man born blind, the Pharisees initiated an investigation to determine exactly what happened,
even though they had already determined the outcome. When
they found facts that did not support their predetermined
conclusions, they kept searching until they found something
that did.

In recording this incident, John recalled the weapons of
the flesh used by the Pharisees:

- *Closed mindedness*—The Pharisees could see the truth
  running counter to their prejudgments, so they simply
  rejected the truth.
- *Discrediting*—The Pharisees asked the man born blind
  about the one who had healed him. When he said it
  was Jesus, a prophet from God, the leaders attempted
  to undermine the credibility of God's anointed.
- *Demands*—The Pharisees demanded to know exactly
  what happened and how it happened, walking by sight
  and not by faith (the opposite of 2 Corinthians 5:7).

Our objective-in-Jesus is to follow the truth, wherever it
leads; we must remember always that the Truth is a person,
Jesus Christ.

HOPEFULLY IN LOVE

And so we know and rely on the love God has for us.
1 John 4:16a

We were singing when I noticed the typo. The lyrics to the praise tune were supposed to be, "I'm hopelessly in love with you." But someone accidentally typed: "I'm hopefully in love with you."

The first suggests an abandonment to love: "God, I'm in this relationship head-to-toe, no matter where it leads." The second suggests tentativeness: "Gee, I hope I can love you, God."

We express a desire to deepen our relationship with God, and there he stands in the deep end calling us to jump in and join him? There we stand, testing the living water with our toes, hesitating to take the plunge that requires fully immersed abandonment to God.

The thing is this: the only thing stopping you from a deep, abiding relationship with God is ... you.

Our objective-in-Jesus is to become hopelessly in love with God. Ask yourself what hinders you from a deeper relationship with God, and ask God to remove any obstacles that are in the way.

OFF-THE-CLOCK CHRISTIANS

I have been crucified with Christ and I no longer live,
but Christ lives in me.
Galatians 2:20

Before dawn, the family-oriented restaurant is slow. I'm the only customer in the place. In a booth a few feet away is a group of employees. Some are on duty, some are just getting off the night shift, and some are not scheduled to work this morning but have come in just to hang out.

As the group talks, one person in particular punctuates his conversation with four-letter words. If this were a movie, the language alone would make it R-rated.

The thing is this: even though some of the employees were off the clock and some were out of uniform, in the *context* of that moment they *all* represented the restaurant.

If we identify with Jesus, he lives in us; there can be no off-the-clock moments when we stop identifying with Christ until the next time we are scheduled to behave as a believer.

Our objective-in-Jesus is to live according to the truth that we have been crucified with Christ; the life we live is no longer ours because Christ lives in us.

The Body in the Basement

When Christ, who is your life, appears,
then you also will appear with him in glory.
Colossians 3:4

My friends were on vacation and they asked me to look after their dog. Coming into their house, I glanced through a window and *that's when I saw the body*.

For a split second, my mind tried to inject logic into what I saw: "Why would Terry and Kathy have a body in their house? Who could it be?" It never occurred to me that something sinister had taken place (1 Corinthians 13:7).

I leaned close to the darkened window and that is when I realized the body was a home gym exercise board covered with a quilt. It had rowing bars folded like arms across a chest and a rest pad for some *body's* feet.

In that fleeting moment I saw a body and I was trying to figure out the mystery of it all. That fleeting moment is like our life on earth. For now we see through the glass darkly—we see only in part—but there will come a day when we will fully understand (1 Corinthians 13:12).

THE LOVE BUCKET

Surely goodness and love will follow me all the days of my life,
and I will dwell in the house of the LORD forever.
Psalm 23:6

Each of us carries a bucket that needs to be filled with love, mercy, and compassion; but when no one fills it for us, we tend to dip into the buckets belonging to others to fill our own.

Faith is believing God will fill your bucket. Faith is also filling the buckets of other people with love from your own bucket, because you trust that God's endless supply of love will keep filling your bucket to overflowing.

This is the cycle of compassion: God gives to us from his inexhaustible supply; then we give to others from the compassion God gives us and they, in turn, fill the buckets of others.

In faith, you can stop your demands for love and attention, and, in faith, you can meet the needs of others, loving them with the love of God flowing through you.

WE ARE BETTER TOGETHER

For we are God's fellow workers;
you are God's field, God's building.
1 Corinthians 3:9

Our diversity is a significant aspect of God's blueprint to create unity in community. We are all together as Christ's body, each of us a "separate and necessary part" (1 Corinthians 12:27 NLT, 1996 ed.).

We see this modeled in congregations every week as people with different talents and abilities work together to prepare for a worship service. Some people are cleaning, others are organizing; some people are preparing to teach, others to greet—all individuals combined as one body to tell others about Jesus.

It is a paradox of our faith that we find our unique and specific purpose in life only after we yield our individualism for the good of many. We become one heart and mind with God and with other believers (John 17:21–22), and in the safety of that community, our true value as individuals emerges.

UNCOMPROMISING ABANDONMENT

"If you love me, you will obey what I command."
John 14:15

When Jesus speaks of love, he allows no room for sentimental fantasy or momentary emotion. He sees love through the eyes of the Father. God-love is bold, strong, and sacrificial.

God plants this love inside us, but it grows healthy in the soil of abandonment. We abandon our rights, our judgments, our opinions, and our schemes. Jesus is uncompromising in his abandonment, saying he says and does *only* what the Father tells him to do (John 14:10). Then, he carried uncompromising abandonment on his back, up the hill called Golgotha.

We too need to abandon anything that sets us in rebellion to the Father. Our thoughts and plans become so close to the Father's that we appear *as one* with him, just as married people, deeply abandoned to each other, appear to live as one.

Jesus says, "If you love me, you will obey what I command" (John 14:15). Open your eyes to this: Jesus isn't reducing love to dutiful acts of obedience; he is saying your love for him should compel you to agree with his plans and to carry out his purposes, not your own.

THIS RIGHTEOUSNESS COAT

I delight greatly in the LORD; my soul rejoices in my God.
For he has clothed me with garments of salvation
and arrayed me in a robe of righteousness.
Isaiah 61:10

Yahweh, by your Grace, I wear a coat of righteousness.

This coat of many godly colors draws attention to the truth that I can do nothing of significance in my own strength. But it also dazzles the world with your compassion and mercy, proclaiming that I can do all things when I wrap myself in you and trust wholly and completely in your strength.

This coat, created by you, keeps me warmly secure in your grace and love. It strengthens me to toss away the rags of self-righteousness in my wardrobe, and it allows me to serve you and others.

This righteous coat keeps me in a position of true humility, knowing whose I am and who dresses me. From this position, I can stand firm before the enemy while also working within the authority you have given me to do your work here on earth.

The more I wear this coat, freely given from you, Father, the more others say I look a lot like Jesus.

GOD LOVING US PERFECTLY

For in Christ all the fullness of the Deity lives in bodily form,
and you have been given fullness in Christ.
Colossians 2:9 – 10

Perfect love desires communion, the sharing of life together, and so it cannot be expressed from a distance. God so perfectly loved the world that he came up-close in Christ, stepping into the brokenness of our lives (1 John 1:1 – 3):

- Into our emptiness, Jesus brings fullness and completion (Colossians 2:9 – 10).
- Into our deficit, Jesus brings supply (Philippians 4:19).
- Into our death, Jesus brings life (Ephesians 2:1, 5).
- Into our separation, Jesus brings reconciliation (Romans 5:10 – 11).
- Into our imperfect love, Jesus brings his *perfect* love (1 John 4:10).

When we know, *and believe*, that God is determined to love us perfectly, we can stop being self-absorbed and we can start being conformed to Christ (Romans 12:2). When we do not believe God is determined to love us perfectly, we end up living like our best choice is to love ourselves.

As a result we become so busy taking care of ourselves that we have little time for authentic, transparent, loving community with others.

GOD-LOVE WALKS ON WATER

We know that we have passed from death to life, because we love our brothers. Anyone who does not love remains in death.
1 John 3:14

Our love for one another is the fruit, not the root, of our relationship with God.

In a sense, the process of sanctification—our movement toward becoming portraits of Jesus—involves God-love cleaning the clutter we have hidden in the cupboards and corners of our being. The Eternal Lover moves with deliberation through the grit and grime of our sin. He throws open the shades and wipes down the windows of our souls until we "shine like stars in the universe" (Philippians 2:15).

As God scrubs our insides with the cleansing blood of Jesus Christ, we pass from "death to life" (1 John 3:14). We are transformed from people who are selective in whom and how we love, into people energized by God's Spirit to love one another abundantly and unconditionally.

Love starts with God. God loved you first, and your ability to love others comes from your connection with God.

Love proves transformation. When you love others abundantly and unconditionally, you prove you have passed from death to Jesus-life (1 John 3:14).

TRUTH: I BRING JOY TO GOD

God decided in advance to adopt us into his own family by bringing us to himself through Jesus Christ. This is what he wanted to do, and it gave him great pleasure.
Ephesians 1:5 (NLT)

In faith, I know this to be true: God is in love with me, and when he thinks of me, it brings him joy.

It was his good pleasure to create me, and he created me so he could love me and his glory could shine through me. He chose me "in him before the creation of the world to be holy and blameless in his sight" (Ephesians 1:4).

His love for me is continuous, so that I can say with confidence and joy, "When I awake, I am still with you" (Psalm 139:18).

By his Spirit, I can live a life worthy of the Lord, and *I am able* to "please him in every way: bearing fruit in every good work, growing in the knowledge of God" (Colossians 1:10).

FORGIVE — AGAIN?

Then Peter came to Jesus and asked, "Lord, how many times
shall I forgive my brother when he sins against me?"
Matthew 18:21

Peter struggled with the dilemma of forgiving a repeat offender and thought he was being generous, under Jewish law, when he suggested to Jesus that he should forgive someone up to seven times.

But Jesus emphasized the *unlimited* generosity of forgiveness by expanding beyond the *limits* of Peter's capacity to forgive; not seven times, but seventy-seven times. God's forgiveness is ever-expanding; we cannot run beyond its borders; we cannot bankrupt the account.

I would hate to think my conversion to Christianity is dependent on being perfect instead of being dependent on God's infinite, indestructible, and immovable grace. There is always a flip side to our conflicts with other people. When we are hesitant to give grace, we forget that we too need grace.

Jesus says we will be judged by the standard by which we judge. Is it seven? Seventy-seven? Or, unlimited?

LOVE INCORRUPTIBLE

*"Greater love has no one than this,
that he lay down his life for his friends."*
John 15:13

Jesus said no greater love has a human being than to lay down one's life for one's friends, but Jesus laid down his life for many more, including enemies, adversaries, and rebels.

His greater love now lives inside us moving us to lay down our lives for others, in the same way Jesus did for us: "I have given you an example to follow. Do as I have done to you" (John 13:15 NLT).

This greater love may not require that we die physically for others, but it does require that we lay down our demands for life on our own terms, our agendas to control, our needs to be noticed.

When others block our demands, frustrate our agendas, or neglect our needs, our tendency is to complain: "God, what are you going to do with these disagreeable people?"

Yet, if we will be still and know he is God (Psalm 46:10), we might hear him respond: "I already did something. I laid down my life for them. Will you do the same?"

TRUTH: GOD COVERS ME WITH HIS STRENGTH

Today I have made you a fortified city, an iron pillar and a bronze wall to stand against the whole land—against the kings of Judah, its officials, its priests and the people of the land.
Jeremiah 1:18

In faith, I know this to be true: By God's hand, I am fortified and I am enabled to fear no one but God.

When I face fear, God whispers in my ear, "Do not be dismayed, for I am your God. I will strengthen you and help you; I will uphold you with my righteous right hand" (Isaiah 41:10).

When standing before fear, I can boldly say, "Who will bring any charge against those whom God has chosen?... Who is he that condemns?... Who shall separate us from the love of Christ? Shall trouble or hardship or persecution or famine or nakedness or danger or sword?... No, in all these things we are more than conquerors through him who loved us" (Romans 8:33–35, 37).

I know this to be true: My God goes before me and comes behind me (Psalm 139:5). He is "my refuge, a strong tower against the foe" (Psalm 61:3).

GOD COMMANDS COMPASSION

"I will have mercy on whom I will have mercy, and I will have compassion on whom I will have compassion."
Exodus 33:19b

Our Creator Yahweh, who "causes to be," has the right to show you compassion, or not.

This does not mean God plays favorites, like, "I will give compassion to the ones I like and leave the others in their misery." It means he has the *right* to decide who gets compassion. It is his call and his decision is final.

We need to understand this point: *we* don't get to decide who gets God's compassion and who doesn't; *we* need to stop telling God how to be God.

Compassion flows from God's nature into us, and it should then flow from us to others. We are just stewards of God's compassion; we don't have the right to withhold God's compassion from others.

Only God has a God's-eye-view, so we are not even in a good position to accurately judge whether God's compassion is wasted. Jesus poured his blood, like a drink offering, into your life: was that compassion wasted on you? How, then, could it be wasted on another?

PUSHING PAST THE PAIN

We always carry around in our body the death of Jesus, so that the life of Jesus may also be revealed in our body.
2 Corinthians 4:10

"Play, even when it hurts" describes a sports philosophy that says you should be so committed in a competition that you don't let the pain from injuries, even some of the major ones, keep you from playing, and playing to win.

In a similar way, Paul sees our pain and heartache — our difficulties in life — as a way to identify with the pain and heartache Jesus faced when he died on the cross for you and me.

Our suffering allows us to experience in a small way, and through the glass darkly, what Jesus experienced when he took on all the brutality, ridicule, and abandonment that was meant for you and me. This is how we carry the death of Jesus around in our bodies, and this allows the life of Jesus to be revealed (2 Corinthians 4:10).

But the good news is that our pain, our heartache, our confusion, our doubts, our mountain-sized difficulties can push us — if we allow them — to the very center of God's all-surpassing power (2 Corinthians 12:7 – 10).

THE LOWLY BABY JESUS

[Jesus], being in very nature God, did not consider equality with God something to be grasped, but made himself nothing, taking the very nature of a servant, being made in human likeness.
Philippians 2:6–7

Most of us approach humility in one of two ways:

- *We act out humility.* We consciously act the way we think humility looks. But by doing this, we live a fabricated humility.
- *We assume we are unworthy.* We assume that we are insignificant, and we live like a Tom Petty-refugee, as if we are somehow second-class.

The biblical approach to humility means you understand exactly who you are, but more importantly you understand *whose* you are. You recognize that God has placed you where he wants you for such a time as this. In this way, your humility is not attached to your self-esteem.

Your objective-in-Jesus is to begin thinking less of yourself while thinking more of God and the power of his love working through you. In your humility he becomes your strength for any task before you.

WHEN REGRET ENTERS OUR SORROW

*The kind of sorrow God wants us to experience
leads us away from sin and results in salvation.
There's no regret for that kind of sorrow.*
2 Corinthians 7:10a (NLT)

From his birth to his death, Jesus lived under difficult circumstances (Isaiah 53:3). Yet, he never shakes a fist at the sky, crying, "What do you want from me? Perfection!?" Not once does he utter regret for his decisions or his life.

Sorrow is part of God's plan, meant to drive us from sin into intimacy with God. We see this in Jesus, who never sinned, on his knees, saying he didn't want the cup but would still do his Father's will. In that moment, "an angel ... strengthened him" (Luke 22:43).

When walking in intimacy with the Father, we have nothing to regret. If regret does enter us, it's a sure sign we are headed from God toward sin. It's the kind of sorrow that says, "I made a mistake that even God cannot make right."

These "if only," "what if" moments can make us feel hopelessly paralyzed. But when we walk with Christ, we make decisions and stick with them, trusting that if we make mistakes, God is big enough to work them out (Jeremiah 29:11; Romans 8:28).

SIN IS ANYTHING
GOD TELLS ME NOT TO DO

You were running a good race.
Who cut in on you and kept you from obeying the truth?
Galatians 5:7

Grace sees sin for what it is: it is anything God tells me not to do. If it breaks the commandment of love, it is sin. If the Holy Spirit checks me and tells me not to go there, but I go anyway, it is sin.

When I let temptation grow into devilish thoughts that take root and grow into behavior abhorrent to God, I have sinned. I then live in a state of unease — *dis-ease* — where my entire being knows that I am not where I am supposed to be and I am not behaving according to who I am in Christ (Acts 17:28).

Like the disciples, I look with heavy eyes at Jesus, asking, "Who then can be saved?"

Jesus looks back in love and says, "With man this is impossible, but with God all things are possible" (Matthew 19:25 – 26).

Sin distracts you from your oneness with God; it pulls you away from your purpose. Instead of trying not to sin, make pleasing God your objective-in-Jesus and you will be less likely to sin.

THINGS WE HAVE IN COMMON

When Jesus reached the spot, he looked up and said to him,
"Zacchaeus, come down immediately. I must stay
at your house today." So he came down at once and welcomed
him gladly. All the people saw this and began to mutter,
"He has gone to be the guest of a 'sinner.'"
Luke 19:5–7

Jesus knew who he was and this allowed him to relax and ignore what others thought or said about him.

It meant Jesus wasn't worried when others accused him of being a friend of sinners, such as Zacchaeus, because he was doing exactly what the Father sent him to do; in effect, teaching others who they were — men and women created in the image of God.

Jesus' actions suggest our witness to nonbelievers starts with friendship: We earn the right to share the gospel through relationship, where we show that we care about the person, not just baptism statistics.

When Jesus met the woman at the well, he pointed to what they had in common rather than the things he could rightfully condemn (John 4). As a result, she not only became friends with God, she brought her friends and family into the presence of Jesus.

Ask God who you are, who he created you to be, and then don't let anybody turn you to the right or left of that truth. Once that is settled, start helping others to discover who they are and what God created them to do.

Truth and Consequences

Do not be deceived: God cannot be mocked.
A man reaps what he sows.
Galatians 6:7

God forgives fully and unconditionally, but that doesn't mean we won't reap what we have sown; the crisis pregnancy remains, the prosecution takes place, the job is lost, or the death occurs.

God brings our sin to light in order to bring us back to him. When God's consuming fire of love forces our bad behaviors and attitudes out of the shadows, we are able to see clearly how far we have moved away from oneness with God and his purpose for our lives.

The crisis that is created when our sins are exposed compels us to journey back to God. It may not feel like it at the time, but God has our best interests at heart, and when we see the big picture, we will be grateful to God for his tough love.

God's desire is not to condemn us, but for us to return to oneness with him. When we see others in sin, rather than condemn them, our objective-in-Jesus is to encourage them back toward oneness with God.

TRUTH: I AM DEEPLY LOVED

*"If you, then, though you are evil, know how to give good gifts
to your children, how much more will your Father in heaven
give good gifts to those who ask him!"*
Matthew 7:11

In faith, I know these words to be true:

God loves me, even more than I love myself. He proved his love for me through the sacrifice of Christ (John 15:13).

God has my best interest in mind, even though it may not appear so at times (Jeremiah 29:11).

My Father knows how to give good gifts. If I, as a human easily led astray, know how to love my children and to give them good gifts, how much more will my Father in heaven lavish on me (Matthew 7:11).

My Lord Jesus says, "Ask and it will be given to you; seek and you will find; knock and the door will be opened to you. For everyone who asks receives; he who seeks finds; and to him who knocks, the door will be opened" (Matthew 7:7–8).

In faith, I believe this to be true.

GOD'S GARRISON OF PEACE?

And the peace of God, which transcends all understanding,
will guard your hearts and your minds in Christ Jesus.
Philippians 4:7

If you lived in a town constantly harassed by enemy raids, one option for your military would be to send troops to actually live beside you. These troops would not only provide protection during an attack; they, hopefully, would dissuade the enemy from even launching any more attacks.

This is the implication of Paul's language in this passage. Jesus became flesh and garrisoned among us (John 1:1 – 14), and now the Holy Spirit garrisons within us.

This garrison of peace mingles and indwells your heart and mind, protecting you even as it heals the wounds of worry and fear that once invaded your life.

It is a peace that passes all understanding because it is God-powered and Spirit-connected: "We have peace with God through our Lord Jesus Christ, through whom we have gained access by faith into this grace in which we now stand" (Romans 5:1 – 2).

YOU ARE ORDAINED BY GOD

You are ... a people belonging to God,
that you may declare the praises of him who called you
out of darkness into his wonderful light.

1 Peter 2:9

The Bible teaches that every Christian, even ordinary people with children and jobs and mortgages and really, really full calendars is ordained by God for ministry.

You are God's instrument "to do his work and speak out for him, to tell others of the night-and-day difference he made for you" (1 Peter 2:9 MSG). What does this mean?

- *God shaped you for ministry.* God calls you to make a contribution to his kingdom, and he has given you unique gifts to work in your area of ministry.
- *God will support you in ministry.* There is no way that you can fail in your ministry unless you fail to accept the calling that comes with being a Jesus-one.
- *God will answer your questions.* Ask God to show you how he will use you to serve him in a way that no one else can. Ask God, "What kind of God-legacy do you want me to leave?"

Hope Not Hype

We have put our hope in the living God, who is the Savior of all men, and especially of those who believe.
1 Timothy 4:10

In a moment of weakness, I bought some *goo* for my boys that I saw advertised on television as lots of fun for creating colorful types of junk.

When it arrived we tried do exactly what the people on TV had done. It will come as no surprise to you that it didn't work. The goo stuck to everything, except the surfaces where it was supposed to stick. My youngest son, in exasperation, said, "They lied to us!"

False hype appeals to our selfish interests, but ultimately undermines our hope and sets us up for disaster.

When we witness to others about who God is and what he is doing in our lives, we are not "hyping goo"; we are telling people that the Holy Spirit will enter their lives and show them what is possible when Jesus is working through them.

Our objective-in-Jesus, then, is to focus "our hope in the living God" (1 Timothy 4:10), letting others know it is God and God alone who transforms them into an image of Jesus.

STUBBORN SELF-IMPORTANCE

Stubbornness [is] as bad as worshiping idols.
1 Samuel 15:23 (NLT)

When we are stubborn, we bow to the idols of self-importance, self-opinion, arrogance, and "I know best."

We say to all, especially to that God who always seems to interfere, that we have established our own inner rule for what is right and wrong.

Jesus was deeply distressed by the stubborn hearts of some Pharisees because they were unteachable, unwilling to learn that people were connected to God through the Spirit and not through the law (Mark 3:5).

They embodied stubbornness by showing more interest in defending a position than in determining the truth. They dug in their heels, allowing the need to win an argument to become their idol. They bowed to the little god of debating little details and little points to the distraction of developing intimacy with the Father.

Exasperated, Jesus finally said, "If you had any idea what this Scripture meant—'I prefer a flexible heart to an inflexible ritual'—you wouldn't be nitpicking like this" (Matthew 12:7 MSG). When you are stubborn, you are in danger of getting everything right, yet ending up completely wrong.

Getting Practical with Love

*Dear children, let us not love with words or tongue
but with actions and in truth.*
1 John 3:18

What you believe inevitably shows up in what you do. If you deeply believe God forgives you, you will be compelled to forgive others. If you believe you are constantly being judged, you are more likely to judge. If you believe the law is the standard for Christian behavior, you will measure others by the law. If you believe the Spirit is the standard for Christian behavior, you will measure others by evidence of the Spirit at work.

Dallas Willard says, "You can live opposite of what you profess, but you cannot live opposite of what you believe."

When we believe God's love is working through us, it will show up in the things we do.

Jesus says love is present when you see the hungry being fed, hospitality being offered, clothes given to those on the streets, care for those who are sick, and concern for those in prison (Matthew 25:35 – 36).

His love is present in you; how does that influence the things that you do?

TRUTH: I CAN TRUST THE TRUTH

"I am the way and the truth and the life.
No one comes to the Father except through me."
John 14:6

In faith, I know these words to be true:

God knows the truth.

The truth comes from God. When the Spirit of truth comes to guide me toward all truth, he will tell me about the truth he has heard from God (John 16:13).

The truth is a person, and his name is Jesus Christ.

Jesus is the truth as spoken by God, the Word from the beginning; the Word that was with God and the Word that was God (John 1:1).

I know the truth: "the glory of the One and Only, who came from the Father, full of grace and truth" (John 1:14).

Jesus does not just teach me truth; he is the Truth (John 14:6).

He Went Away Sad

When the young man heard this, he went away sad,
because he had great wealth.
Matthew 19:22

In this age of sound bites and gotcha journalism, there is fear that one wrong word or choice will define us, regardless of a lifetime of right words and right decisions.

In the same way, the rich young ruler is remembered for the moment "he went away sad" because he could not make an unconditional commitment to Jesus. Yet, what is so quickly forgotten is that the young man was a committed believer with a life significant for its godly behavior and kingdom work.

He was not a defiant, rebellious follower, hell-bent on having his own way; he was a devoted follower, no different from you or me. But what Jesus asked, what the Lord required, was too much for him.

He was unwilling to cross the chasm between "I can" and "I can't," a chasm with a bridge built on the whip-scarred back of Jesus, the Christ. The man was holding back some of his trust, some of his faith, just in case he needed to fall back on "I must."

Downloading God's Vision

He persevered because he saw him who is invisible.
Hebrews 11:27

God reveals his vision a little bit at a time. He doesn't show us his entire vision at once because often we are not ready to understand it, or because we will be overwhelmed with its magnitude and frozen by our doubts.

In a sense, God reveals his vision like a slow download from the Internet, like a picture that appears on your computer screen in stages.

God gave Moses the vision of deliverance, but he didn't map the whole plan immediately. Moses left Egypt, he confronted Pharaoh, he led the children of Israel across the Red Sea, and he kept them moving for forty years through the wilderness until they reached the Promised Land.

Moses "persevered because he saw him who is invisible." And God's slow download of his vision strengthened Moses' faith, as he waited for each part to appear.

Guided by the Holy Spirit within and by God's purpose before us, our objective-in-Jesus is to persevere toward God's vision, even if we are unable to see the full picture ahead.

HEAVENLY INSIGHT

Let us fix our eyes on Jesus,
the author and perfecter of our faith.
Hebrews 12:2

As we become one with God, he draws us into his eternal perspective, where we see life is more than just the here and now. We move from simply saying that the things of God are true to living in radiant certainty that they are true.

Jesus looked beyond the cross and could see the glory on the other side. He received heavenly insight from the Father that enabled him to see past the hardship, enabling him to endure the cross with a radiant certainty of God's faithfulness.

The enemy wants to keep your focus on the things below, but Jesus, the author writing the story of our faith, keeps pointing to the things above, where we will meet a joy-filled future, forever and ever. Amen!

His message is that you too can be radiantly certain of God's commitment to your best, and so when things go wrong—at your job, with your relationships, in your bank account, with your health—you can view these hardships as opportunities to fix your eyes on Jesus.

PROVING JESUS IS WITHIN

"A new command I give you: Love one another.
As I have loved you, so you must love one another."
John 13:34–35

We are the salt of the earth, but we lose our saltiness when we lose our love (Matthew 5:13). And the whole world is watching how that love plays out, particularly from one believer to another. If people filled with Jesus-life can't get along; if they can't show the most basic tenets of love for each other, then why should the world be interested at all in being filled with the life of Jesus?

If we let Jesus' love flow through us and flood the lives of those within our Christ-community, then the world will see a love so authentic and contagious that it will attract them to Jesus in us.

People are not attracted by a list of rules, but they are attracted by streams of living love that flow from Jesus through us into the lives of those we meet (John 4:10; 7:38).

If you want to prove to others that Jesus' love is in you, then love others just as Jesus loves you.

REARVIEW MIRROR

For you did not receive a spirit that makes you a slave again
to fear, but you received the Spirit of sonship.
Romans 8:15

Mr. Smith, a better than average driver, is cruising down main street. He has done nothing wrong. He is under the speed limit and his registration is up-to-date. Yet, when he glances in his rearview mirror and sees a police car following him, he gets nervous.

The policeman doesn't have his lights on, his siren isn't wailing, and he doesn't appear to have his eyes on Mr. Smith. But Mr. Smith's anxiety grows.

He starts thinking through a mental checklist of anything he might have done wrong. Was I speeding? Did I cut somebody off? Did he see me roll past that stop sign? Is my taillight out? Why didn't I buy those tickets for the policemen's ball! Finally he watches the policeman pull past him and speed down the road.

Mr. Smith is a snapshot of us when we continue to live in fear of the law even after God's grace has entered our lives. "Perfect love drives out fear, because fear has to do with punishment. The one who fears is not made perfect in love" (1 John 4:18).

FRIENDS WHO STICK CLOSE

*A man of many companions may come to ruin, but there is
a friend who sticks closer than a brother.*
Proverbs 18:24

It's a stone-cold fact that many people find closer relationships among friends than they do among their blood relatives. But there is a different type of blood relative, sisters and brothers who are grafted together through the blood of Jesus Christ. His power within us gives us the ability to become companions who stick together closer than a brother or sister.

This requires considerably more commitment than our standard "to each his own" approach to getting along. Instead, we agree there will be "none of this going off and doing your own thing" (Colossians 3:15 MSG).

We see each other as individuals, unique creations of God and vessels of God's grace. We "develop a healthy, robust community that lives right with God and enjoy its results" when we "do the hard work of getting along with each other, treating each other with dignity and honor" (James 3:18 MSG).

ONE SPIRIT TO GUIDE US

But he who unites himself with the Lord
is one with him in spirit.
1 Corinthians 6:17

With one Spirit guiding us, we can learn to rely on the holy logic of Christ and learn to think like Jesus. We no longer need to understand everything because we know that our perfect God is in control and that our imperfect perceptions are not based on the full reality of his omniscient plan (Proverbs 3:5; 14:12; 1 Corinthians 2:15–16).

We look to God to tell us what is true, knowing that our feelings, and even our thoughts, do not determine the truth. We look to God, knowing that the opinions of others—even a majority—do not have the final say on what is true. Truth is what God says it is, and God alone holds the authority for interpreting any situation or circumstance (2 Corinthians 10:5; 13:8; 1 John 4:1).

Our courage and confidence to overcome the Devil, sin, and the fallen world is *in Christ* and his truth.

STEP WITH THE SPIRIT

Since we live by the Spirit, let us keep in step with the Spirit.
Galatians 5:25

Sometimes the Spirit leads us to greater restriction than the law requires: "where others can; we cannot." At other times, the Spirit may direct us to do more than the law requires, as foreshadowed by Jesus: "If a soldier demands that you carry his gear for a mile, carry it two miles" (Matthew 5:41 NLT).

If we are led by the Spirit, we are no longer under the law (Galatians 5:18). We are compelled by love instead of law, by faith instead of fear.

The fruit of the Spirit's work within us is "love, joy, peace, patience, kindness, goodness, faithfulness, gentleness and self-control. *Against such things there is no law*" (Galatians 5:22–23, italics added).

The law is meant to drive us to dependence on the Father and submission to the Holy Spirit, whom he has placed within us.

JESUS' HEART, FILLED WITH COMPASSION

When the Lord saw her, his heart went out to her and he said, "Don't cry." Then he went up and touched the coffin ... "Young man, I say to you, get up!" The dead man sat up ... and Jesus gave him back to his mother.

Luke 7:13 – 15

Two blind men were sitting by the roadside, shouting, "Lord, have mercy on us!" Jesus asked, "What do you want me to do for you?" They answered, "We want our sight." And Jesus, with compassion, touched their eyes. Immediately they received their sight and followed him (Matthew 20:30 – 34).

A man with leprosy came to Jesus, saying, "If you are willing, you can make me clean." Filled with compassion, Jesus reached out his hand and touched the man. "I am willing," Jesus said. "Be clean!" Immediately the leprosy left him and he was cured (Mark 1:40 – 42).

In all such stories, what action does Jesus take to show compassion? Ask God to show you how to make this kind of compassion practical in your life.

An Ambassador
Knows the King

We are therefore Christ's ambassadors,
as though God were making his appeal through us.
2 Corinthians 5:20

"Thank you so much for pulling together this little soiree so we could meet and greet. I'm honored to be the new ambassador, here to represent the King and all his interests.

"Some of you have asked me about the King—what he's really like—and I have to tell you, I've never met him. In fact, I really don't even know the King, only what other people have told me and a few things I memorized when I was a boy.

"But, don't let that concern you, I have no doubt I will serve the King well as his ambassador to … excuse me, you there, what country is this again?"

Your intimacy with Jesus is what allows you to be an ambassador for him. Because you know him—*intimately*—you know about his passions and you can answer from his wisdom. The key to effective evangelism is not in method, but in knowing Jesus deeply.

Becoming Familiar
with Suffering

He was despised and rejected by men, a man of sorrows,
and familiar with suffering.
Isaiah 53:3

For us to become like Jesus, God will acquaint us with sorrow. God's intent is not to hurt us, but to expand our capacity to carry his love into a world in desperate need of compassion. The sorrows we experience become part of the Holy Spirit's work within us. Through them, God transforms us into beings of love who "shine like stars in the universe" (Philippians 2:15).

Sorrows clarify our thinking and help us trust that God is at work within and around us. In this way, "we always carry around in our body the death of Jesus, so that the life of Jesus may also be revealed in our body" (2 Corinthians 4:10).

But even as Christ's death is at work in us, so also is his life. He began a good work in us that will be carried on "to completion until the day of Christ Jesus" (Philippians 1:6).

BIRTHDAY

*Therefore we do not lose heart. Though outwardly we are wast-
ing away, yet inwardly we are being renewed day by day.*
2 Corinthians 4:16

On my most recent birthday, my sister sent me this
message:

"The bad news: 'Therefore we do not lose heart, even
though outwardly we are wasting away.'"

Did I mention that this is my *older* sister, and as I like to
remind her, she will always be my *older* sister? She added to
her message:

"The good news: 'Even though outwardly we are wasting
away, yet the inward man is being renewed day by day.'"

We may be wasting away on the outside, but our spirits are
renewed day by day and our connection to God never grows
old. If you have creaky joints, arthritic hands, weakened eyes,
a slow step, an ear that struggles to hear, or a heart that beats
to the sound of a cholesterol drummer, be encouraged!

God is preparing a grand birthday celebration for the day
you arrive in heaven, where you will no longer age because
you'll be home among the ageless.

DEALING WITH ANOTHER'S HISTORY

Be completely humble and gentle; be patient,
bearing with one another in love.
Ephesians 4:2

Developing patience comes through the learned skill of seeing other people the way God sees them. Practicing patience teaches us to keep looking toward the things above, even in the most difficult of circumstances or with the most difficult of people.

The apostle Paul wrote, "Welcome with open arms fellow believers who don't see things the way you do. And don't jump all over them every time they do or say something you don't agree with ... Remember, they have their own history to deal with. Treat them gently" (Romans 14:1 MSG).

- *Patience comes with practice.* Most people can be patient when it is convenient; the real test comes when time is slipping away or when someone keeps repeating the same mistakes.

- *Patience comes with cost.* Patience requires that you trust God's timetable and set aside your rights and demands, using the sacrificial strength that comes from Jesus' love within you.

- *Patience comes through God's love.* Patience may cost you all the love you have, but that's okay! God will give you more because his supply is endless.

GOD IS STRONG;
HE WANTS YOU STRONG

At once the man was cured; he picked up his mat and walked.
John 5:9

For thirty-eight years the man was paralyzed in a sickly cycle of passive dependency, hoping to make it to the end of each day, longing for something else. Circular survival thinking of this kind traps us in a death-like state where we are ruled by our fears, far removed from the abundant life Jesus promised.

Then Jesus said, "Get up! Pick up your mat and walk."

He told the man he had other options: "You can get up and walk, step into faith, and leave behind your fear. God is strong, and he wants you strong."

The paralytic had thirty-eight years of experience telling him his legs would not support him. He had no experience in trusting this man named Jesus. But then, he took one step of experience telling him Jesus might be right, two steps telling him Jesus could be right, three steps telling him Jesus must be right, four steps telling him Jesus was absolutely right.

What of us? Will we do whatever God tells us to do to be healed?

Do Not Limit Your Service to Others

*"For who is greater, the one who is at the table
or the one who serves? Is it not the one who is at the table?
But I am among you as one who serves."*
Luke 22:27

As a new creation in Christ, you no longer need to be motivated by fear. You are now free to view life in terms of what is best for others. This activates the fruit of the Spirit, which represents love in its many flavors: joy, peace, patience, kindness, gentleness, faithfulness, self-control.

When God and his loving nature become your point of reference, you should start asking: "What is God's best for others in this situation?" This will inspire you to offer a quality of service to others far beyond what you are likely to give if you only offer them your ideas of what is best.

Our service is enabled by God's "mighty power at work within us" that is able "to accomplish infinitely more than we would ever dare to ask or hope" (Ephesians 3:20 NLT, 1996 ed.).

Here's the thing: don't allow your vision of the possibilities for serving others be limited to your own strengths and resources.

ETERNALLY IMPORTANT PERSONS

Each one of us needs to look after the good of the people around us, asking ourselves, "How can I help?" That's exactly what Jesus did. He didn't make it easy for himself by avoiding people's troubles, but waded right in and helped out.
Romans 15:2–3 (MSG)

It is not uncommon to serve people who, by earthly standards, seem to be important. But the Bible turns this around, explaining that the starting point for servanthood is to consider *everyone* an E.I.P. (Eternally Important Person).

As Jesus-ones, we no longer judge others by their looks or personality or wealth or position; instead, we see in their faces their resemblance to the Father, who created each one of them in his image. When we see everyone as important, it becomes natural to ask, "How can I help you?"

C. S. Lewis says that every human being is an eternal being; the question is where he or she will spend eternity. When we begin to see everyone as an E.I.P., then, like Jesus, we can lovingly enter their lives and help them find the bridge to eternity with God.

A Father's Heart: Otherly Love

"Love your neighbor as yourself."
Luke 10:27

The Bible teaches that you should act deliberately to show love toward your neighbor — in the same way you want your neighbor to love you. God knows this is an impossible assignment unless you have his Spirit within you, guiding and transforming you.

You will be empowered to love your neighbor as you allow God to empower you; as you purposefully give your whole being — heart, soul, strength, and mind — to God.

This brings you daily to the door of dependence on God. It leads you to a threshold that you step through acknowledging that you need him to work through you. In doing this, you are able to draw on God's strength and love; he becomes the power and the infinite love within you to love others as yourself.

They may waste your love, they may discount your love, they may react angrily to your love, they may never understand your love; yet, your other-centered love demonstrates the depth and breadth of God's love for us. "While we were still sinners, Christ died for us" (Romans 5:8).

FREE TO LIVE FREE

For God did not give us a spirit of timidity,
but a spirit of power, of love and of self-discipline.
2 Timothy 1:7

Making our way down a list of rules appeals to our pride; it nurtures the notion that we can earn God's favor through our own efforts. The thing about following lists is that they keep a bit of fear in the room even as God is chasing this anti-faith emotion out the door with his perfect love.

The spirit God places within us has his courage and uncommon boldness. It is not a spirit of timidity. Timidity is based on the false belief that terrible things will happen if we make a mistake. It is a sin rooted in passive legalism that proclaims we have got to do the right things in the right way at the right time, perfectly every time, or we will be in trouble with God.

That is a lie with the smell of hell all over it because Jesus paid for every one of our mistakes and there is no fear in God's perfect love (1 John 4:18).

"Go Where You Wanna Go"

Your attitude should be the same as that of Christ Jesus.
Philippians 2:5

Back in the carefree 1960s, we were taught to do whatever we wanted, anywhere we wanted, and with anyone we wanted.

If we are transparent, is it possible that this is the way we live, even though we have Jesus within us? We affirm our faith, but we tend to go where we wanna go, do what we wanna do, with whomever we wanna do it with.

The apostle Paul taught the early church a different song. Imagine these lyrics projected on the first-century version of a JumboTron: "My attitude will be like Jesus' attitude." Jesus agreed he wouldn't go wherever he wanted, whenever he wanted; instead, he agreed to do and say only what the Father told him to do and say (John 5:19).

When I read these lyrics, I confess I have been singing about my own selfish attitudes and not the other-focused attitudes of Jesus Christ, my Lord.

Gentle Jesus-one, what song are you singing today?

GOD AT WORK ON HUMAN LIFE

*"I have set you an example that you should do
as I have done for you."*
John 13:15

Fred was under my car. It needed new brake pads and I couldn't afford to pay a mechanic. The car had a rusted undercarriage and smelled of mildew, but I was grateful just to have some form of transportation.

In the heat and smudged with grease, Fred steadily kept at it, even when we realized almost all the parts we needed to detach were rusted together and required ingenuity and brute force to take them apart.

And as we worked, we talked. We shared our stories of the faithful, hopeful, loving Christ and how he had transformed our lives. I was humbled by Fred's genuine humility as he worked under my car.

Fred was my pastor and the love of Jesus in him was not passive, but rolled up under the brake drums of a 1973 Pontiac LeMans. Fred's example was an echo of Jesus, who after washing the disciples' feet, said, in essence, "Look at my life — this is what God at work in a human life looks like" (John 13:12 – 17, author paraphrase).

WAR, BY GOD'S METHODS

*We demolish arguments and every pretension that sets itself up
against the knowledge of God, and we take captive
every thought to make it obedient to Christ.*
2 Corinthians 10:5

Use today's devotional as a prayer:

Father, teach me to wage spiritual war according to your
manner and not the world's. Guide me to live with *weapons
of the Spirit* and not weapons of the flesh.

Be my strength, Lord, when I am up against the wall.
Lord, train me so that when I face conflict, discouragement,
or temptation I rely on you and follow your way.

Your truth says you have given me the power and authority to demolish arguments and every pretension that sets itself
up against the knowledge of you.

So, rather than getting into arguments, Lord, make
me ready to use the tools you provide and show me how to
"demolish arguments and every pretension that sets itself
against" you. Show me how to take every thought captive
and make it obedient to Christ. I commit to doing what you
teach me to do.

May this be so, my Lord.

GOD SPOKE YOU INTO EXISTENCE

*"Before I formed you in the womb I knew you,
before you were born I set you apart; I appointed you
as a prophet to the nations."*
Jeremiah 1:5

Dear one, you were born because the God of the universe first imagined you!

The God who spoke the world into existence, the God who hung the moon and the stars, the God who set the sun in the sky—this creative Creator thought about you, was pleased by his thoughts, and so he spoke you into your mother's womb.

You were created by God at just the right time, in just the right place to serve God in "such a time as this" (Esther 4:14). You are a unique creation, like a priceless painting from a grand master (Ephesians 2:10 NLT).

If you have been rejecting yourself, then you have been rejecting God's design of you. It's okay to talk to him about your frustrations, disappointments, or confusion.

Ask God to give you a clear and constant vision of who you were created to be; then, ask him to be your strength and wisdom as you live it out.

GOT YOUR NOTE OF DOUBT

Therefore I will boast all the more gladly about my weaknesses,
so that Christ's power may rest on me.
2 Corinthians 12:9

Hi! I got your note saying you don't think you can do what God is telling you to do.

You may be surprised to hear me say this, but I agree! If God called you to do it, then you shouldn't be able to do it without him. If you could do it without him, then it's not really a "God thing." Your weaknesses, doubts, and insecurities are no surprise to God. You may try to hide them from others, but you cannot hide them from the one who created you.

Is it possible that God created you with weaknesses in order to keep you on your knees before him? This way, you are able to do all things through *him* who strengthens you (Philippians 4:13).

God won't let you use weaknesses as an excuse for *not* doing what he is asking you to do. He did not call other people to this task; he called you and in his strength you can do it.

HOOKING OUR HOPE

*Consider it all joy ... when you encounter various trials,
knowing that the testing of your faith produces endurance.*
James 1:2–3 (NASB)

When God tells us to count it all joy when we go through
trials and tribulations, you have to wonder if he has forgotten
what it is like to live below the clouds.

A number of years ago my daughter, Kathryn, died. My
wife and I were angry with God. We had asked him to save
Kathryn and it seemed he did not answer our prayer. But God
showed us that our perspective was extraordinarily narrow.
We had placed our hope in the answer we demanded, instead
of trusting that God knew what he was doing. We had hung
our hopes on the wrong hook, forgetting that God's hope will
not disappoint (Romans 5:1–5).

Paul is not saying we cannot or should not grieve; rather,
he is saying that death or any other loss is not the end of
the story because we serve the God of Glory. We believe
Jesus died and rose again, and that God will resurrect those
in Christ who have been taken from us, so we can encourage one another with these words of hope (1 Thessalonians
4:13–18).

OBJECTIVE-IN-JESUS:
GROWING BY KNOWING

"We believe and know that you are the Holy One of God."
John 6:69

When the well runs dry, we know Jesus is the river of living water (John 4).

When the storm rages, we know Jesus is the Lord of the storms (Matthew 14).

When the floods overwhelm, we know Jesus is the rock on which to build (Matthew 7).

When the foundation shivers, we know Jesus is the cornerstone that will not move (Matthew 21).

When sickness comes, we know Jesus is the healer (Matthew 4).

When we are bankrupt through the debt of sin, we know Jesus is our redeemer (Galatians 3).

When we grieve, we know Jesus is the voice calling from the shore, "Friends, haven't you any fish?" (John 21).

When we are full of doubt, we know Jesus is the nail-scarred palm inviting our touch (John 20).

Jesus taught in the context of everyday life because he knew disciples with focused faith are never made in the classroom.

We are transformed in the midst of uncertainties, when what we know of God takes root and changes the way we live. We change because we have believed and come to know firsthand the "Holy One of God" (John 6:69).

IDENTIFIED AS GOD'S

He has identified us as his own by placing
the Holy Spirit in our hearts.
2 Corinthians 1:22 (NLT)

Your faith will grow stronger as you focus on your identity in Christ (Galatians 2:15 – 21). If you don't know who you are, you are vulnerable to other people telling you who you are. But the concrete, solid, gospel truth is that you are who God says you are. No one else has a vote in the matter.

This "identity issue" is an important part of living the abundant life. Jesus was able to face the incredible demands of his mission because he knew exactly who he was; he knew that he mattered to God, and that gave him confidence to move purposefully in faith.

Your objective-in-Jesus is to develop a deep, deep understanding about the truth that you are God's precious child and he created you in a way that pleases him. Ask God to give you insight into why you struggle to see yourself identified with Christ and ask him to reveal why you doubt the power of the Holy Spirit within you.

IN HIS GRIP

So be careful to do what the LORD your God has commanded you; do not turn aside to the right or to the left.
Deuteronomy 5:32

Occasionally, I sign my letters with the words, "In his grip." I started doing this during a tough period in my life. God showed me that he had me in his grip with a strength that would never let me go.

Wrapped in the strength of his grip was the calling he would place on my life. I kept trying to get away, but in a sense, "When I kept silent, my bones wasted away through my groaning all day long" (Psalm 32:3).

Even before he placed you in your mother's womb, God had a plan for you. He created you for a purpose, to be a voice for him in this specific time and place. And that is why "I'm absolutely convinced that nothing—nothing living or dead, angelic or demonic, today or tomorrow, high or low, thinkable or unthinkable—absolutely nothing can get between us and God's love because of the way that Jesus our Master has embraced us" (Romans 8:38–39 MSG).

"In his grip."

CHRIST-BODY COMPANIONS

So in Christ we who are many form one body,
and each member belongs to all the others.
Romans 12:5

God created you to live and grow within a Christ-body, a place where Christians share life and share the love of the Father with the rest of the world — together, not in isolation.

Let's say you are a hand in the Christ-body — clearly you have an important role, but you won't be able to handle all the things God planned for you if you are not connected to the arm, the shoulder, and the head.

You are that dependent. You are also that unique. The truth that some of us are hands, and others are eyes, and others are legs, and so on, is proof that God designed us to live life together. Think, then, in terms of ministry and mission. You don't have to do them alone. You can do them together with a group of Jesus-ones, each one doing what God shaped him or her to do.

Our objective-in-Jesus is to live within this truth: Collectively, we are not just the hands and feet of Jesus; when we work together as a body of believers, we are his whole body working in ministry to others.

JESUS AND THE
BROOKLYN DODGERS

Therefore do not let anyone judge you by what you eat
or drink, or with regard to a religious festival,
a New Moon celebration or a Sabbath day.
Colossians 2:16

On *Saturday Night Live* comedian John Belushi performed a skit where he led an American combat patrol. Coming upon a person who was possibly a German spy, Belushi asked something like, "Who plays shortstop for the Brooklyn Dodgers?" The man couldn't answer, so Belushi put him at gunpoint.

Someone in Belushi's squad asked, "Hey, Sarge, who does play shortstop for the Dodgers?"

"Camenker, you must be a German spy too." Belushi ordered him to stand with the German prisoner. And so it went until the only person left on the trigger side of the rifle was Belushi.

"Hey Sarge, who does play shortstop for the Dodgers?"

Belushi blurts out, "Oh man, I don't know! I must be a German spy too!" And he joins the others.

We keep excluding people based on jot-and-tittle questions, such as what they eat or drink, how they celebrate a holiday, or if they wear a tie on Sunday (Colossians 2:16). God comes in grace, saying, "The only thing that counts is faith expressing itself through love" (Galatians 5:6).

My Children Walk in Truth

I have no greater joy than to hear that my children are walking in the truth.
3 John 4

Being a pastor is one of the toughest jobs on the planet, but John says there is "no greater joy" (3 John 4).

Spiritual leaders must correctly teach God's Word, confront false teaching before it spreads, proclaim the gospel to unbelievers, pray for all people, and train and appoint leaders —all while serving as an example of what it looks like when you are maturing as a Jesus-one (see 1 and 2 Timothy; Titus).

The apostle Paul says, "Obey your leaders and submit to their authority. They keep watch over you as men who must give an account. Obey them so that their work will be a joy, not a burden" (Hebrews 13:17).

Pray for your spiritual leaders today, that they continue to walk in the truth, and let them know in some way that you want to bring them joy by "walking in the truth" with them.

ON THE NIGHT BEFORE YOU DIED

*"Watch and pray so that you will not fall into temptation.
The spirit is willing, but the body is weak."*
Matthew 26:41

On the night before you died, you prayed for me, that I would be as close as a heartbeat to the Father (John 17:22).

On the night before you died, you called me friend, no longer a servant, because you had taught me everything the Father taught you (John 15:15).

On the night before you died, you came to me with bloody sweat dripping down your face and arms because you had stared straight into the future with eyes wide-open. I hid behind the covers of my deep sleep, in denial.

On the night before you died, you shook me and seemed to ask, "Can't you watch *with* me? Come beside me, friend, and wait *with* me" (Matthew 26:40, author paraphrase).

On the night before you died, you understood my struggle, but never demanded that I understand yours. You whispered, "I know how it is, brother, 'the spirit is willing, but the body is weak'" (Matthew 26:41).

NO SMALL DREAMS

"I found a good hiding place and secured your money.
Here it is, safe and sound."
Matthew 25:24–25 (MSG)

Rick Warren once said, "If you're not making mistakes, then you're not trying anything new." His point was that we should not be afraid to risk failure because there should be no small dreams for those belonging to God.

In Matthew 25, three servants were given talents. The first two invested and doubled their amount, but the third buried his in a hole, in essence saying, "I don't want to take any risks."

When the master found out, he responded: "That's a terrible way to live! It's criminal to live cautiously like that! If you knew I was after the best, why did you do less than the least?" (Matthew 25:26 MSG).

There's another word for risk-taking: faith. If we are not taking any risks—if we are walking in a way that does not require faith—then we are being faith-*less*.

Jesus said, "Everything is possible for him who believes" (Mark 9:23).

SWEET SACRIFICE

Live a life of love, just as Christ loved us and gave himself up
for us as a fragrant offering and sacrifice to God.
Ephesians 5:2

When Mary used her hair to rub perfumed oil between her Savior's toes, Jesus suggested that such a great sacrifice leads to great influence: "I tell you the truth, wherever this gospel is preached throughout the world, what she has done will also be told, in memory of her" (Matthew 26:13).

Perhaps Jesus could smell the sweet fragrance of Mary's sacrifice because he knew that love finds meaning in sacrifice: "We understand what love is when we realize that Christ gave his life for us. That means we must give our lives for other believers" (1 John 3:16 GWT).

Paul reminds us that God gives us the grace required to become living sacrifices. God places the Holy Spirit in us to make us holy and pleasing to him (Romans 12:1).

Our objective-in-Jesus is to "live a life of love, just as Christ loved us and gave himself up for us as a fragrant offering and sacrifice to God" (Ephesians 5:2).

A God Not Made
by Our Own Hands

He burns part of the tree to roast his meat ...
Then he takes what's left and makes his god.
Isaiah 44:16–17 (NLT)

In 1980, Howard Cosell interrupted a Monday night football game with the announcement that John Lennon, a member of the Beatles, had been murdered outside his New York City apartment.

In an eerie moment, ABC Sports respectfully cut sound from the game just as a play broke on the field. Television viewers, numbed by the news, sat in silence while fans at the game, unaware of Lennon's death, cheered wildly.

As I grieved, a Bible verse floated into my mind: "For what will it profit a man if he gains the whole world, and loses his own soul?" (Mark 8:36 NKJV). I would like to tell you that I fell to my knees and forever turned from my prodigal path. In my arrogance, I continued to wander a long and winding road to the Truth.

The prophet Isaiah spoke about men who fashioned a god out of wood, a god unable to deliver them. So, by their own hands, they were doomed.

Our objective-in-Jesus is to rid ourselves of any gods we have fashioned from our own hands and serve the one true God.

PEOPLE WITH INTEGRITY

The man of integrity walks securely,
but he who takes crooked paths will be found out.
Proverbs 10:9

People with integrity live by fairness, even when fairness puts them at a disadvantage or causes them significant difficulty. They fight fair even when those around them do not.

People of integrity consider their word their bond, allowing their "yes" to mean yes and their "no" to mean no.

People of integrity are authentic and transparent; they act the same, no matter who is present.

People of integrity are straightforward in their conduct. They don't hide what they are doing, or say one thing and do another. They are people "in whose spirit is no deceit" (Psalm 32:2).

People with integrity explain the facts in an even-handed manner; they don't try to present things in a way that makes them look better at the expense of another. They are respectful, helpful, and gracious to everyone and anyone.

People of integrity focus on "whatever is true, whatever is noble, whatever is right, whatever is pure, whatever is lovely, whatever is admirable," anything at all that is "excellent or praiseworthy" (Philippians 4:8).

SERVE EACH OTHER EAGERLY

Do not use your freedom to indulge the sinful nature;
rather, serve one another in love.
Galatians 5:13

Being free and being a servant sounds like a contradiction; servants are rarely free. But the apostle Paul teaches that freedom and service are intertwined.

Once we were slaves to sin (Romans 6:6). We had no choice but to focus on our own needs and wants (Ephesians 2:1 – 2). But Jesus broke the bondage of sin and now we are free to look for the spontaneous opportunities the Holy Spirit creates for us to do something for someone else.

Your objective-in-Jesus is to become eager to serve: pay attention to those around you so you can become sensitive to their needs. "Each one of us needs to look after the good of the people around us, asking ourselves, 'How can I help?'" (Romans 15:2 MSG).

THE FAITH OF WORKS

Faith by itself, if it is not accompanied by action, is dead.
James 2:17

Consider this paraphrase (based on James 2:14, 17): "Dear brothers and sisters, what's the use of saying you love your spouse if you don't prove it by the way you treat your spouse? That kind of impersonal love doesn't make your relationship a marriage. A book-learned love that doesn't show up as an open-armed, hands-on love is no love at all."

This helps us see the holy union of faith and works. I can say I love my spouse, but unless I do *good works* within my marriage, it is hard to spot my love. Yet, it is possible for me to go through the motions of good works, even if I have little love for my spouse.

Your good works emerge from your spirit-connection to God; they are not independent of God's power and love. It requires faith to do what God requires of us, to enter the lives of others in order to show them the uncommon compassion of Jesus.

THE FORGETFUL SERVANT

*"I have set you an example that you should do
as I have done for you."*
John 13:15

It is nearly impossible to remain self-centered while serving the deep needs of another person. Paul says, "In humility consider others better than yourselves" (Philippians 2:3).

Jesus set an example for us when he *got up* from the meal and then *got down* on his knees to wash his students' feet (John 13:4–5).

Since people wore sandals or walked barefoot on dusty roads, they needed to clean their feet when they entered a house. Usually, a servant would do the dirty chore, but Jesus assigned the service to himself, "taking the very nature of a servant" (Philippians 2:7). Menial work was not beneath Jesus.

Serving others begins with forgetting yourself (Matthew 10:39). With your own needs out of the way, follow Jesus' example and look for the other person's needs. "Now that I, your Lord and Teacher, have washed your feet, you also should wash one another's feet" (John 13:14).

Ask God to show you one relationship that would be transformed if you emphasized the other person's needs over your own.

THE INVASION OF PRAYER

He was appalled that there was no one to intervene.
Isaiah 59:16

Most of our prayers are of the low order — maybe more like a fast-food order. We pull up to the drive-through and yell out our requests to God. When we get to the window we expect him to have our order ready.

God's view of prayer seems far above the utilitarian view of prayer. He calls us to a violent form of intercession, where we take on the spiritual forces of darkness on behalf of our people, once invaded, now occupied by the prince of darkness.

We think about others and pray for them like Jesus would think and pray for them. We cover them with prayer, protect them through prayer, and advocate for them in the same way Jesus sits at the right hand of the Father and advocates for us (Romans 8:34).

This is other-centered prayer on the extreme end of "other." Today, try to pray at least an equal amount for others as you do for yourself.

THE MINISTRY OF ACCEPTANCE

*So from now on we regard no one from
a worldly point of view. Though we once regarded Christ
in this way, we do so no longer.*
2 Corinthians 5:16

Growing up, I considered my older brother, Cole, the embodiment of cool. I often wished I could be like him. Just about everyone seemed to accept and like him.

One summer I stayed a few weeks with my brother. While we were at a restaurant with his friends, Cole said, "I think Jon would fit in well with our group." Those words are some of the most meaningful words ever spoken to me. My cool brother was telling me I was accepted, and his cool friends agreed with him.

You may have felt the sting of rejection, but the good news is that Jesus doesn't care what you have done or where you have been. He knows all your secrets—and he still accepts you!

In his ministry of acceptance, Jesus sees every person as an individual—valuable, important, and created by God. When you begin your ministry of acceptance, what will that look like in your life?

THE VICTORY LAP

Do you not know that in a race all the runners run, but only one gets the prize? Run in such a way as to get the prize.
1 Corinthians 9:24

Have you ever wondered why the winner of an Olympic marathon runs a victory lap? Here is an athlete who just ran twenty-six consecutive miles, without a break for lunch or a stop at Starbucks, and the reward is to run a lap around the stadium, waving at the crowd.

Come on! If I win a marathon — and there is little chance of that — I think I would say, "Strap me in a recliner, start giving me Gatorade intravenously, and push me around the stadium. Hey, go get the guy who comes in last to push me; he's the one who should be running an extra lap!"

All kidding aside, my friend, we run the race for "a crown that will last forever" and therefore, we do not run aimlessly (1 Corinthians 9:25 – 26).

Thanks to Jesus our champion, our victory is assured — in truth, already won. The glory goes to God, forever and ever, amen.

TRUTH: GOD GIVES ME HIS PEACE

I am not saying this because I am in need, for I have learned to be content whatever the circumstances.

Philippians 4:11

By faith, I hold this to be true: God takes care of me. When I stay close to him, I can be content "whatever the circumstances."

He shows me that contentment "is not a matter of eating and drinking, but of righteousness, peace and joy in the Holy Spirit" (Romans 14:17). This joy and peace gives me overflowing hope in him by the power of the Holy Spirit (Romans 15:13).

Jesus gives me his peace. The contentment I find *in Christ* is greater than anything the world has to offer. Contentment with Jesus is a treasure beyond imagination. I need not be troubled or afraid because Jesus is always with me (John 14:27; 1 Timothy 6:6).

I know these things to be true because Jesus told me, "In this world you will have trouble. But take heart! I have overcome the world" (John 16:33).

TOUGH TATTOOED LOVE

Three things will last forever—faith, hope, and love—
and the greatest of these is love.
1 Corinthians 13:13 (NLT)

There is a woman with words of love tattooed across her back. Etched in her skin is the entire thirteenth chapter of 1 Corinthians, what we so often refer to as the love chapter.

The astonishing thing is that the woman is not even a Jesus-one; she is simply into that nebulous concept of universal love that poets and idealists speak of so easily.

Jesus also bore tattoos upon his back, etched by thirty-nine lashes from a nail-tipped whip. The body piercings in his hands and through his feet were made by horrific Roman railroad-like ties. They were thick enough to pin all our sin upon him, our Savior and Redeemer.

This ruthless love is specific, sweaty, and sincere. It is tattooed on our hearts in God's own script by the suffering of Jesus, the author and perfecter of our faith. His love energizes us to endure opposition, so that others will not grow weary and lose heart (Hebrews 12:3).

Treasures in the Darkness

I will give you the treasures of darkness, riches stored in secret places, so that you may know that I am the LORD, the God of Israel, who summons you by name.
Isaiah 45:3

God gives us dark times in order to give us treasures in the darkness. He wants us to know deep within that, if God is not God in times of trouble, then he isn't God at all. Instead of trying to avoid the pain in our lives, God wants us to see that the pain in our lives is often a path toward maturity, where we grow confident that God is God even and always in times of trouble.

The apostle Paul says suffering produces such godly treasures as perseverance, character, and hope. "And hope does not disappoint us, because God has poured out his love into our hearts by the Holy Spirit, whom he has given us" (Romans 5:5).

Our objective-in-Jesus is to faithfully believe God will use our suffering to make us more like Jesus.

Trust Me, I'm a Reporter

Now an angel of the Lord said to Philip,
"Go south to the road—the desert road—
that goes down from Jerusalem to Gaza."
Acts 8:26

There is an old joke about a beginning reporter sent to do a story about a town meeting. He comes back a few hours later covered in soot and tells his editor there is nothing to report because the town hall burned to the ground: "Some of us barely got out with our lives!"

The young reporter missed a far more important story because he didn't understand that journalists must be willing to drop everything they are doing at a moment's notice in order to chase a new story that is a higher priority.

Philip was on the way back to Jerusalem when God told him to take a different route. In his obedience, he found God already working within the treasurer of Ethiopia. From this conversation an entire nation learned about Jesus.

We need to develop a similar flexibility. When God disrupts your plans, his agenda takes priority over yours. Ask God to give you discernment in these moments and to help you develop obedience.

MAKE THE HOLE YOUR GOAL

Until we ... become mature,
attaining to the whole measure of the fullness of Christ.
Ephesians 4:13

When I used to played golf, my main goal was to reach the green without majorly embarrassing myself, so I was satisfied when my ball made it somewhere near the fringes.

One day, a golf pro told me the key difference between an average golfer and one who is excellent is that the truly great players shoot directly for the hole. Not somewhere near the hole or somewhere on the green, they aim directly for the hole.

He told me, "You should make the hole your goal." I didn't think I would ever be able to hit the hole, so I wouldn't even try.

The reason so many of us are unable to move into deeper intimacy with God is because we don't think it is possible. So we don't even try. But the Bible says it is possible to mature, even until we attain "the whole measure of the fullness of Christ" (Ephesians 4:13). Don't settle for a relationship with God that is on the fringe of the green; shoot directly for the hole and watch how God draws you near to him.

Truth: I Am Becoming Like Jesus

Those who belong to Christ Jesus have crucified the sinful nature with its passions and desires.
Galatians 5:24

In faith, I know these words to be true:

God is developing my character and, through the Holy Spirit, he's planted the character of Christ in me. He's more concerned about growing a Jesus-like character in me than he is with my convenience or comfort, which are fleeting things at best (Galatians 5:24).

God initiates my growth into the character of Jesus by freely giving me his salvation. He creates within me a willing spirit so that I can teach others about God's compassion (Psalm 51:12–13). God's objective is to complete the fullness of joy within me (John 15:11).

As God grows me in Christ, I begin to have my Father's eyes of compassion that enlighten me "in order that [I] may know the hope to which he has called [me], the riches of his glorious inheritance in the saints" (Ephesians 1:18).

WILL GOD HELP YOU?

You see, at just the right time, when we were still powerless,
Christ died for the ungodly.
Romans 5:6

You probably agree that God is the supreme ruler of the universe, powerful enough to overcome any problem or defeat any enemy, and that "everything comes from him; everything happens through him; everything ends up in him" (Romans 11:36 MSG). If this is true, then when you struggle to trust God, the issue is not about his ability to fulfill a promise—he clearly can do that.

Your doubt may be more like, "Yes, I believe God can work this out, but will he?" Or, "I think I know how to work this out, but I'm not sure God does, at least I'm not sure he will do it the way I want to see it done."

God patiently understands your hesitancy. He made the first move toward establishing a trusting relationship with you. He did not wait until you could be trusted to receive his love, and he does not insist you become trustworthy before he trusts you with precious gifts (Romans 5:6–8). You learn to trust God by obeying him in small ways each day.

WITHOUT FORGIVENESS,
FELLOWSHIP IS IMPOSSIBLE

*Be kind and compassionate to one another, forgiving
each other, just as in Christ God forgave you.*
Ephesians 4:32

Whenever someone hurts us, we have a choice to make: we can focus on retaliation or resolution, on getting even or giving grace.

Truth is candid about settling the score: "Make sure that nobody pays back wrong for wrong, but always try to be kind to each other and to everyone else" (1 Thessalonians 5:15). God will take care of any payback, but he will approach it with the same grace that he extended to you—Christ died for you while you deserved payback (Romans 5:8; 12:17–21).

It is not enough to say we won't seek revenge; we are to press into the very heart of forgiveness, forgiving each other, just as Christ forgave us. God sets this high standard because he knows how much is at stake. Bitterness and unforgiveness are a cancer that will eventually destroy you from the inside out and damage the transformation God is working in you.

Which would you rather have growing inside you: the cancer of unforgiveness or the healing transformation of God?

YOU ARE GOD'S GREAT IDEA

When I was woven together in the depths of the earth,
your eyes saw my unformed body.
Psalm 139:15 – 16

God spoke my son, Jeremy, into my wife's womb, just as God spoke you into your mother's womb. Jeremy was "fearfully and wonderfully made," and God ordained his days, just as he has ordained yours (Psalm 139:14, 16).

Jeremy died at birth because of a disorder called Trisomy 18, but that didn't diminish the value of his life, his legacy, or his significance to God.

If you grasp "how wide and long and high and deep is the love of Christ" (Ephesians 3:18), you will understand how each individual is a masterpiece created by God. You are of immeasurable worth to God, and your value is not determined by your appearance, how much time or money you can contribute, what you do, or how long you live. The value of any container is determined by its contents, and you are a one and only, custom-made container filled with the very life of God. Rejoice in this truth and be set free.

TRUTH: I HAVE GIFTS FROM GOD

It was he who gave some to be apostles, some to be
prophets, some to be evangelists, and some to be pastors
and teachers, to prepare God's people for works of service,
so that the body of Christ may be built up.
Ephesians 4:11 – 12

In faith, I know these words to be true:

God is working in me and he has given me the gifts I need to work for him. I have talents from God and his blessings to use them, for I am his "workmanship, created in Christ Jesus to do good works, which God prepared in advance for [me] to do" (Ephesians 2:10).

God has given me "the Spirit of wisdom and revelation" so that I may know how to use my gifts. He has enlightened my heart so that I may know the inheritance of his hope. He has placed his power within me through the Holy Spirit and "that power is like the working of his mighty strength" (Ephesians 1:17 – 19).

In faith, I will live accordingly, because I know these words to be true.

MINISTRY AS LOVE

The only thing that counts is faith expressing itself through love.
Galatians 5:6

Mary said, "I am the Lord's servant ... May it be to me as you have said" (Luke 1:38). And God said, "The only thing that counts is faith expressing itself through love."

"Why do you eat and drink with tax collectors and 'sinners'?" (Luke 5:30). Because the only thing that counts is faith expressing itself through love.

"Love your enemies, do good to those who hate you" (Luke 6:27). Show others the only thing that counts is faith expressing itself through love.

"Master, if you'd been here, my brother wouldn't have died" (John 11:21 MSG). May you see in this moment that the only thing that counts is faith expressing itself through love.

"When he had received the drink, Jesus said, 'It is finished'" (John 19:30). The only thing that counts is faith expressing itself through love.

"Peace be with you! As the Father has sent me, I am sending you" (John 20:21). Go with peace, knowing the only thing that counts is faith expressing itself through love.

Mr. Miyagi and the Karate Kid

A gentle answer turns away wrath,
but a harsh word stirs up anger.
Proverbs 15:1

When people come at us angry, we tend to push back in anger. We may match their intensity or even escalate the conflict.

No doubt you have seen situations where the original offense was relatively minor, but one angry reaction piled on another pushed the argument nuclear! Maybe, like me, you have even been a part of one of those arguments.

James, the half brother of Jesus, writes to us saying, "Be quick to listen, but slow to speak" (James 1:19 GWT). James echoes the wisdom of Solomon, which whispers across the centuries: "A gentle answer turns away wrath, but a harsh word stirs up anger" (Proverbs 15:1).

Think of it this way: when you come up against anger, do what Mr. Miyagi told the Karate Kid to do. Match rage with control and confront threats with compassion. Exercise your faith by responding in peaceful ways: lower your voice instead of raising it, smile instead of frowning, and find agreement instead of magnifying your differences.

TRUTH: GOD KNEW ME
BEFORE I WAS BORN

From birth I was cast upon you;
from my mother's womb you have been my God.
Psalm 22:10

In faith, I know these words to be true:

Before I was formed in the womb God knew me (Jeremiah 1:5). He "created my inmost being" and "knit me together in my mother's womb" (Psalm 139:13).

From birth I have relied on God; he brought me forth from my mother's womb. I will ever praise him, my God and heavenly Father (Psalm 22:10; 71:6).

I am God's workmanship, created in Christ Jesus to do good works, which God prepared in advance for me to do (Ephesians 2:10). My objective-in-Jesus is to live dependent on God, regardless of my feelings, thoughts, or any peer pressure that would pull me away from God's purpose for me.

Lord, I will trust you with all my heart; I will not lean on my own understanding. You straighten the path before me, Lord; I will acknowledge you in all my ways (Proverbs 3:5–6).

EMPOWERED TO REBUILD LIVES

Administer true justice; show mercy and compassion to one another. Do not oppress the widow or the fatherless, the alien or the poor. In your hearts do not think evil of each other.
Zechariah 7:9–10

The Holy Spirit empowers you to love others with such godly compassion that they can begin to rebuild their lives. God guides us to:

- *Pursue justice.* We show compassion when we act as a voice for those who have no voice.
- *Extend mercy.* When we show mercy to those in the wrong, it means we recognize he or she is a flawed human, just like us, in need of salvation.
- *Express kindness.* We can show kindness, even to those with whom we disagree. We can model civility and respect.
- *Give others the advantage.* Instead of focusing on getting a greater advantage, we can use what advantage and privileges we do have to help others.
- *Protect vulnerable people.* Our compassion compels us to look out for the interests of others, in particular, those in volatile or vulnerable situations.

CRAVING GOD

"Return, faithless people; I will cure you of backsliding."
Jeremiah 3:22

When was the last time you craved intimacy with God, wanting it so badly you chased after it with abandonment? If you are like me, you may wonder if you can love God with such an everlasting, overpowering love again. You may be thinking, "God, I don't think that kind of love is humanly possible!" If that is what you are thinking, you are right. Only God is able to change the desires within you; he is able to rekindle a deeply devoted love within you.

If you have lost your passion for God, the way to get it back is not to try harder until you somehow reach that level of love. You can have it back by asking God to fill you with his holy love.

God will forgive our prodigal nature. He will cure us of our lethargic faith: "Return, faithless people; I will cure you of backsliding." The people of Israel responded immediately, "Yes, we will come to you, for you are the LORD our God" (Jeremiah 3:22). As we are and from where we are, Lord, we come.

UNCOMMON SAFETY

Whoever lives in love lives in God, and God in him.
1 John 4:16b

God enables us to drive fear away from our families and friends by loving one another so supportively that everyone feels safe inside the group—by living in community. This safety allows us to bring our humanness into the open, including our pain and joy, our ups and downs, our victories and defeats, our fears and faith (1 John 4:18).

The New Testament shows that this kind of God-energized support means we help others reach their full potential in Christ (Colossians 3:13–16; 1 Thessalonians 5:11–15).

With this uncommon authentic support, we can laugh together and weep together. We can comfort and confront, warm and warn, cherish and challenge, all within an atmosphere of Christ-centered safety that loves the fear out of one another (1 Corinthians 12:25–26; 1 Peter 1:22; 1 John 4:16).

THE HARD WORK OF REST

There remains, then, a Sabbath-rest for the people of God; for anyone who enters God's rest also rests from his own work.
Hebrews 4:9–10

It's late at night as my father lifts me from the backseat of the car. I slip into slumber because I'm safe at home, resting in my father's arms, and he will soon put me into my bed where I can sleep until morning.

This is one of the most powerful memories from my childhood, and it personifies our Sabbath-rest with God. We can rest in the Father's arms, confident and worry-free because the Father carries us.

This is the rest of "be still, and know that I am God" (Psalm 46:10). It is the rest of faith, where our only work is "to believe in the one he has sent" (John 6:28). In this rest, you no longer work for God; rather, you let God work through you. Rest now in God's power and grace, knowing he is who he says he is and he will do what he says he will do.

Is God Waiting on You?

God also said to Abraham ...
"I will bless [Sarah] and will surely give you a son by her."
Genesis 17:15 – 16

Just like you or me, Sarah and Abraham may have thought, "God doesn't understand our circumstances; his commandments are good guidelines, but they simply don't work well in the nitty-gritty of life." So they took matters into their own hands, and Hagar gave birth to Ishmael. But God had promised that *Sarah* would deliver a son for Abraham. So they continued to wait, long after reaching the point of desperate frustration — until they were ready to say, "God, we can't go on any longer!"

You've been there. Like the widow knocking on the judge's door, you have prayed day and night but the door remains shut (Luke 18:1 – 7). Sarah and Abraham knocked on that door for another fourteen years! (Genesis 16:16; 21:5).

They were wholly dependent on God to fulfill his promise. Not dependent because they had obediently submitted everything to him, but totally dependent because they had exhausted every other possibility.

And that's often why God delays. He is waiting on us to be ready for him.

COMING TO A MESHACH MOMENT

But even if he does not ... we will not serve your gods.
Daniel 3:18

Faced with a fiery furnace, Shadrach, Meshach, and Abednego told King Nebuchadnezzar, "Our God may rescue us. He may not rescue us, but that doesn't matter because he is still our God and we will worship only him" (Daniel 3:16–18, author paraphrase).

These three faithful servants taught me about devoted service at a time when I was agitated because God seemed to delay his provisions for an urgent need. I was angry and demanded God provide on my timetable.

Finally, I realized there was absolutely nothing I could do to make this thing happen. I was totally and wholly dependent on God to fulfill his promise.

It was then I had what I have come to call my "Meshach moment," when I finally said, "God may provide for me. He may not provide for me, but that doesn't matter because he is still my God and I'll serve him no matter what."

Could God be steering you toward a "Meshach moment," bringing you to a place where you are faithful even if God's answer is slow in coming?

No Curses in Heaven

Do not repay evil with evil or insult with insult,
but with blessing, because to this you were called
so that you may inherit a blessing.
1 Peter 3:9

It will take some getting used to, but there will be no curses in heaven. We may find it strange, at first, to be in a place where there is no criticism, faultfinding, or mean-spirited judgment. We are so immersed in the language of insults and put-downs that we have become numb to its effect on us all.

The New Testament teaches our objective-in-Jesus should be to stop sounding like Satan, the accuser, and to start speaking in the language of love, encouraging each other into the fullness of Christ (Matthew 7:1–5; Romans 14). Our objective-in-Jesus is to develop the habit of speaking well of others. We bring out the best in them as they respond to the love of God flowing through us.

When we bless one another, we draw attention to the One from whom all blessings flow. We experience only a taste of heaven here on earth, whetting our appetites for the full banquet yet to come.

A MISSION OF DRUDGERY

For Christ's love compels us, because we are convinced
that one died for all, and therefore all died.
2 Corinthians 5:14

A friend of mine in a difficult marriage told me one thing he had learned is that physical intimacy flows from emotional intimacy. It is the overflow of a deep, abiding love between two people wholeheartedly committed to each other.

Although a painful lesson, he said he now understands that God wants us on-mission because we love him. He wants our participation to be an overflow of our intimacy with the Father.

Otherwise, our mission will, sooner or later, evolve into drudgery. We will head out on-mission because we have to do our Christian duty, or we will avoid it altogether because it seems too difficult and tedious. And in the process, we very likely will teach others about a god who demands as opposed to a God who is love (1 John 4:8).

Our objective-in-Jesus is to allow our intimacy with God to compel us into our purpose, and our first step toward purpose is to develop intimacy with the Father.

AND THAT'S THE HONEST TRUTH

*Therefore each of you must put off falsehood and speak
truthfully to his neighbor, for we are all members of one body.*
Ephesians 4:25

Being honest in Christian community means you no longer use pretense to keep others from seeing the real you.

"We refuse to wear masks and play games ... we keep everything we do and say out in the open, the whole truth on display, so that those who want to can see and judge for themselves in the presence of God" (2 Corinthians 4:2 MSG).

Honesty deepens our relationships, allowing us to be transparent with one another (Proverbs 24:26). It keeps our fellowship open and authentic, freeing us to speak the truth in love as we practice remarkable integrity (Ephesians 4:15; Titus 2:7).

It keeps us sensitive to the Holy Spirit's guidance and helps us battle deceptions that corrupt our lives in Christ (John 16:13; 2 Corinthians 10:5).

Make it your goal today to tell others the truth. "In Christ's body we're all connected to each other ... When you lie to others, you end up lying to yourself" (Ephesians 4:25 MSG).

GOD IS STRONGER
THAN WE THINK

I can do everything through him who gives me strength.
Philippians 4:13

We are not as strong as we think we are, and God is stronger than we think. You become strong through God's strength. His strength enters your life, delivered by the Holy Spirit. The more dependent you are on God, the stronger you become in him.

"I can do everything" doesn't mean, "Now that I'm a believer, I'm strong enough to do everything and anything for God." The strength of "I can do everything" comes from God, who gives you the strength you need for each day. Your ability to "do everything" is wholly dependent on him because your *strength* is dependent on him.

In faith you can act in confidence, knowing that God is giving you his strength: "But the Lord stood at my side and gave me strength" (2 Timothy 4:17).

It will take all of your strength to admit your weaknesses before God, and to submit yourself to him completely.

OBJECTIVE-IN-JESUS:
TRUTH SPEAKS IN LOVE

*Instead, speaking the truth in love, we will in all things
grow up into him who is the Head, that is, Christ.*
Ephesians 4:15

When Truth enters the room, he speaks in the language of love. His words do not demand; his words do not control. His words sweep in like freedom pouring hope into your soul. His language offers life, "like a tree planted by streams of water, which yields its fruit in season and whose leaf does not wither" (Psalm 1:3).

When others sound like an annoying repetitive gong or like the clattering of a cymbal, Truth speaks in love with words cushioned in tender, patient kindness (1 Corinthians 13:1).

When Truth speaks in love, he knows no word for envy or for rudeness. His tongue gets tied; he's unable to speak in pride.

When Truth speaks in love, he is not self-seeking, or easily angered, and he keeps no record of wrongs. The voice of truth "always protects, always trusts, always hopes, always perseveres" (1 Corinthians 13:5, 7).

If the voice of truth doesn't speak in love, then it isn't speaking truth.

No Particular Thing We Seek

Therefore I do not run like a man running aimlessly.
1 Corinthians 9:26

The Carpenter was working in his shop one afternoon when he noticed a band of brothers walking by. It struck him as odd because the same group had passed by his shop twice in the last hour. He offered them water and asked about their journey. "Oh, we're not on a journey," the collective said. "We're on a quest."

"What do you seek?" asked the Carpenter.

They said, "We don't really know what we seek. Yes, it could be a leak. Or, it could be something sleek. It may be to become meek."

"But, if you don't know what you're seeking, how will you know when you find it?"

"It doesn't matter," said one named Zeek. "We just seek." And on that beat, they moved down the street.

If we don't know what we seek, then we risk seeking the wrong things first (Matthew 6:33). If we don't know whom we seek, then we may not realize he is right there in front of us: "You will seek me and find me when you seek me with all your heart" (Jeremiah 29:13).

SAINTS OF SACRIFICE

We must give our lives for other believers.
1 John 3:16 (GWT)

Service cannot be separated from sacrifice. As Christians, we must shift from giving little or no sacrifice to being willing to sacrifice any and all that may be required to help others.

King David understood that service is sacrifice and would not offer a sacrifice to God that cost him nothing: "But the king replied to Araunah, 'No, I insist on paying you for it. I will not sacrifice to the LORD my God burnt offerings that cost me nothing.' So David bought the threshing floor and the oxen and paid fifty shekels of silver for them" (2 Samuel 24:24).

The cost of sacrificial service is beyond mere notions of money. It may mean giving up dreams, expectations, reputations, retirements, whatever God asks in order to lovingly enrich the lives of others.

We benefit today because saints before us served by sacrificing. It is now our time to do the same for others, living like the poetic King David, who served his generation before he died (Acts 13:36).

FORGIVENESS ISN'T THE SAME AS STUPID!

*"But I tell you: Love your enemies
and pray for those who persecute you."*
Matthew 5:44

Forgiving those who hurt us does not mean excusing their behavior and it does not mean we have to stay in an abusive relationship. My sister says it bluntly: "Forgiveness isn't the same as stupid!"

To echo the civil rights activist, Dr. Martin Luther King Jr., we need to understand the difference between nonviolent resistance and nonresistance to evil. In any toxic relationship, we resist the evil of abuse without resorting to evil ourselves.

We submit, not to the abuse, but to God, who draws us into a Spirit-directed response. He wants us to establish healthy boundaries that make us less vulnerable to abuse when we are behind them. You may need distance and time to trust again. You may need to wait, and see how faithful the one who hurt you is to rebuilding trust.

Although it may seem you are paralyzed in an abusive situation, you can make choices. One choice is to pray for those who abuse you. Our objective-in-Jesus is to learn to love our enemies and to develop an ability to pray for those who persecute us.

MISSIONS AS TRUTH

This Good News tells us how God makes us right in his sight.
This is accomplished from start to finish by faith.
Romans 1:17 (NLT)

When we go on mission for God, we tell others that Truth is a person, God's son Jesus, and that God is love.

We report what we have seen and what we have heard, what God has done, what he will do in our lives, and what he has done in the lives of others (Matthew 11:4–5).

We carry God's truth to those who have "exchanged the truth of God for a lie," by worshiping and serving "created things rather than the Creator" (Romans 1:25).

We tell them of a never-ending love so powerful it defeats all fear, all hatred, all injustice, and all sin.

We proclaim "that the Son of God came so we could recognize and understand the truth of God . . . and we are living in the Truth itself . . . Jesus Christ . . . both True God and Real Life" (1 John 5:20 MSG).

I Can't Like It

We should no longer be slaves to sin — because anyone
who has died has been freed from sin.
Romans 6:6–7

When my son was two years old, he would sometimes push away food, making a face while saying, "I *can't* like it," as if he didn't have a choice.

It's a cute phrase coming from a child, but not so cute when we say the same thing to God: "Sorry, Lord, I can't do that because I *can't* like it." What we really mean is "I *won't* do it."

We tell God we can't change, we can't handle a difficult situation, we can't abandon a bad habit, and we can't learn to love someone who irritates us. What we really mean is we won't control our anger, we won't stop overeating, and we won't love our neighbors as we love ourselves.

We act as if we have no choice; yet the apostle Paul says we are free to walk in godly obedience. We can choose to say no to sin, relying on the Holy Spirit's strength to help us make godly choices.

LIGHT FOR THOSE
AVOIDING CHRISTMAS

The virgin will be with child and will give birth to a son,
and will call him Immanuel.
Isaiah 7:14

I sit in a fast food restaurant observing a young girl celebrating an early Christmas with her mother. Her presents are spread out across the booth and she says, "I miss you, Mommy."

"I miss you too, baby," her mother says.

Beyond their booth I see a woman casually, but carefully, watching them. She is a social worker supervising a structured visit for mother and child, who are doing the best they can to celebrate Christmas. A few minutes later, the foster parents arrive to take the girl home with them while the mother leaves alone.

There is a darker side of Christmas that we rarely acknowledge. There are many of us whose Christmas dreams rarely match reality, whose memories are full of tension, not tinsel.

For those tired of the hollow hope and the false fantasies of Christmas, the good news is that God is with us. A virgin gives birth to a son, and his name is Immanuel (God with us).

We Wait for the Seasons to Change

But if we hope for what we do not yet have,
we wait for it patiently.
Romans 8:25

Between October 1 and January 1, I have been to so many family funerals and waited in so many hospital waiting rooms that I'm honestly relieved when the ghost of Christmas is truly past each year.

I know I am not alone in feeling that the promise of "on earth peace, good will toward men" (Luke 2:14 KJV) sometimes violently collides with the reality of broken dreams and irretrievable relationships.

We wait for the season to change, and I cannot say I always wait with Spirit-infused grace, but the changing seasons are a consistent reminder of his faithfulness: the seasons come and go as surely as the sun will rise tomorrow, and God, by setting the seasons in motion, whispers, "Year in and year out, you trust the seasons to return; now trust me to be just as faithful."

This season in your life will change; there *will* be new life. Jesus *did* walk out of the tomb on the third day; he *is* resurrected and alive. He conquered death, so he can handle any situation you may be facing today.

GOD ENGINEERS A CENSUS

*In those days Caesar Augustus issued a decree
that a census should be taken ... And everyone
went to his own town to register.*
Luke 2:1, 3

Jesus was born in Bethlehem because God decreed it. His birth was foretold by the ancient prophets. But what would compel Joseph and Mary to travel from Nazareth to Bethlehem, especially late in a pregnancy?

In Luke 2, we see God used a bureaucratic announcement made by a secular authority to guide Joseph and Mary. Augustus said the population should be counted, and that meant everyone was required to return to their "ancestral home." Joseph was a descendant of King David, so he headed toward David's ancient home, Bethlehem (Luke 2:4–5).

Just as God engineered the circumstances of Jesus' birth, he continues to engineer circumstances around us every day.

How would you view the circumstances of this Christmas season differently if you were certain God was working "to give you a future and a hope" (Jeremiah 29:11 NLT)?

Blind Truth: The Seeing Man

*"The man they call Jesus made some mud and put it on
my eyes. He told me to go to Siloam and wash.
So I went and washed, and then I could see."*
John 9:11

A sign of our spiritual maturity is when we follow truth wherever it leads, face the truth no matter how much it hurts, and stand on truth no matter how much it costs. When the now-seeing man saw the truth, his whole perspective changed.

We see truth with Jesus-eyes. The blind man now had eyes that could see, and he saw with Jesus-eyes. Yet, his neighbors couldn't believe their eyes. They were blind to the ways of Jesus: "The man without the Spirit does not accept the things that come from the Spirit of God, for they are foolishness to him, and he cannot understand them" (1 Corinthians 2:14).

We testify oneness-with-God. As the now-seeing man walked back from Siloam, those who had ridiculed him saw a man transformed. His abandonment to God transformed him into a new man; Jesus re-created him from a man born blind to a man who could see to eternity.

TRUTH: I CAN BE ALL THERE

Give your complete attention to these matters. Throw yourself into your tasks so that everyone will see your progress.
1 Timothy 4:15 (NLT)

You have probably heard the story of the guy on a long drive with his wife. As she talked, his mind began to drift until it vaguely registered she had just asked him a question. He looked at her and she repeated, "So, what do you think I should do?"

He took a deep breath, and said, "Well, what do you think?"

Glaring, she said, "You weren't listening to me, were you?"

Our objective-in-Jesus is to be fully present, in the present. We look life full in the face and engage all our senses in what is around us, especially the people we encounter.

We don't let the past distract us, and we don't let the future worry us; we remain focused in the present. We value those around us enough to put down the newspaper, look up from the computer, turn off the TV, and really listen to them.

Our objective-in-Jesus is to begin *being all there* in the present, so we can be sensitive to the needs, hurts, likes, dislikes, and the many joys of those around us.

OPENING PACKAGES

God is able to make all grace abound to you,
so that in all things at all times, having all that you need,
you will abound in every good work.
2 Corinthians 9:8

As my six-year-old tried to open a package, I sat patiently waiting for him to ask me for help. It was one of those hard plastic packages that are nearly impossible to open.

I knew my son wouldn't be able to open the package on his own, but I wanted him to make his own choice about whether or when he would ask me for help. It didn't take long before he looked up at me and asked for help.

Today, you may be holding a package in your hand that is wrapped in a hard plastic shell — inside is a gift, what Jesus calls the "abundant life." You may be straining to open the package, using anything you can think of to get inside.

Meanwhile, God is patiently waiting for you to abandon your attempts to create the abundant life and say, "I can't, but God, you can." He is waiting for you to let him loose in your life so he can become your strength.

"THY" SALVATION

Restore unto me the joy of thy salvation;
and uphold me with thy free spirit.
Psalm 51:12 (KJV)

It is easy to misread this verse: "Restore unto me the joy of *my* salvation." The difference between "my" and "thy" may seem like simple semantics, but the chasm between the two is so vast that there is only one bridge capable of spanning the gap: Jesus' arms spread wide on the cross.

"My" salvation means I do it myself. I have a right to my salvation. It is mine, and it's all about me. "Thy" salvation means we have no right to it, and we cannot earn it. It is a gift from God, his to bestow based on his love, his promise, his sacrifice, and his grace. This is the good news that brings great joy (Luke 2:10).

Otherwise, the good news is not so good if it's based on "my" instead of "thy." If our salvation is based on what we do, then we will always wonder if we have done enough. But if our salvation is based on the grace of God, then we can always know enough has been done.

Jesus says, "It is finished" (John 19:30).

USING GOD'S WEAPONS

For our struggle is not against flesh and blood,
but against the rulers, against the authorities,
against the powers of this dark world and against
the spiritual forces of evil in the heavenly realms.
Ephesians 6:12

When we face conflict, God provides the tools we need to respond as Jesus would respond. Paul calls these tools "weapons of the Spirit," saying we should respond with them rather than react with "weapons of the flesh."

Satanic weapons, what Paul refers to as faithless weapons of the flesh, are strategies, tactics, and methods we use to get our own way, or to get our needs met without the help of God (2 Corinthians 10:4–5). These weapons include manipulation, gossip, slander, ridicule, threats, blame, nagging, deception, and silence.

Weapons of the Spirit include truth, righteousness, peace, faith, salvation, and God's Word (Ephesians 6:10–20). Also in the Spirit's arsenal are, "love, joy, peace, patience, kindness, goodness, faithfulness, gentleness and self-control" (Galatians 5:22–23).

Our objective-in-Jesus is to stop using faithless weapons of the flesh and start using weapons forged by God to cooperate with the Holy Spirit. What one *flesh weapon* will you lay down today?

"It Is Finished"

Jesus said, "It is finished." With that,
he bowed his head and gave up his spirit.
John 19:30

When Jesus died on the cross, his work of redemption was complete. Matthew and Mark say he gave out a loud cry as he died, but John adds the detail of what Jesus said in that moment: "It is finished."

His words could be rendered, "It is paid in full!" Jesus paid the required price for our sins, bringing us back into communion with God. There is no other work required, nothing we need to pay in addition to what Jesus has done.

Picture this: Jesus gives a victory cry, as if he hears his Father say, "It's done, well done!"

Jesus shouts with joy, "It is finished!" The victory is won; the captives are free to come home. To signify that the gap between sinful human beings and the holy God has been bridged forever, the "curtain of the temple was torn in two from top to bottom" (Matthew 27:51; Mark 15:38; Luke 23:45).

The victory is won; you are free to abide with God, his Spirit alive in you.

A Resolution worth Keeping

For I resolved to know nothing while I was with you except Jesus Christ and him crucified.
1 Corinthians 2:2

How are you doing with your New Year's resolutions? You remember that list you made with optimistic enthusiasm but unrealistic expectations?

One of my friends started making New Year's resolutions such as, "I won't lose ten pounds this year," and "I commit to watching the Super Bowl this year."

I suspect Paul only had one resolution on his list: "This year I resolve to know nothing but Christ and him crucified." Paul's message is radically simple: salvation is in Christ alone. What does this mean?

- It's not Christ plus your good behavior.
- It's not Christ plus the number of Bible verses you memorize.
- It's not Christ plus your tithe or the church you attend.
- It's not Christ plus wisdom from the latest Christian seminar.

It's simply Christ plus nothing. Christ and Christ alone.

Copyright Notices of Scripture Versions Used

CEV   Scripture quotations marked CEV are taken from the *Contemporary English Version*. Copyright © 1995 by American Bible Society. Used by permission.

GWT   Scripture quotations marked GWT are taken from the *God's Word® Translation*. Copyright © 1995 by God's Word to the Nations. Published by Green Key Books. Used by permission.

HCSB   Scripture quotations marked HCSB are taken from the *Holman Christian Standard Bible*. Copyright © 1999, 2000, 2002, 2003 by Holman Bible Publishers. Used by permission.

TLB   Scripture quotations marked TLB are taken from *The Living Bible*. Copyright © 1971 by Tyndale House Publishers. Used by permission.

MSG   Scripture quotations marked MSG are taken from *The Message*. Copyright © 1993, 1994, 1995, 1996, 2000, 2001, 2002. Used by permission of NavPress Publishing Group.

NASB   Scripture quotations marked NASB are taken from the *New American Standard Bible*. Copyright © 1960, 1962, 1963, 1968, 1971, 1972, 1973, 1975, 1977, 1995 by The Lockman Foundation. Used by permission.

NJB   Scripture quotations marked NJB are taken from *The New Jerusalem Bible*, copyright © 1985 by Darton, Longman & Todd, Ltd. and Doubleday, a division of Bantam Doubleday Dell Publishing Group. Used by permission.

Sources Used

Bonhoeffer, Dietrich. 1995. *The Cost of Discipleship*. New York: Touchstone.

Chambers, Oswald. 1992. *My Utmost for His Highest*. Grand Rapids, Mich.: Discovery House.

Guthrie, Nancy. 2007. *Holding On to Hope: A Pathway through Suffering to the Heart of God*. Wheaton, Ill.: Tyndale House.

Kushner, Lawrence. 1998. *The Book of Words: Talking Spiritual Life, Living Spiritual Talk*. Woodstock, Vt.: Jewish Lights.

Lewis, C. S. 2001. *Mere Christianity*. New York: HarperCollins.

Merton, Thomas. 1999. *The New Man*. New York: Farrar, Straus and Giroux.

Nouwen, Henri J. M. 1994. *The Return of the Prodigal Son: A Story of Homecoming*. New York: Doubleday.

Peterson, Eugene H. 1983. *Run with the Horses*. Downers Grove, Ill.: InterVarsity Press.

———. 1988. *Traveling Light: Modern Meditations on St. Paul's Letter of Freedom*. Colorado Springs, Colo.: Helmers & Howard.

Thomas, Major W. Ian. 2006. *The Indwelling Life of Christ: All of Him In All of Me*. Sisters, Ore.: Multnomah.

Warren, Rick. 2007. *The Purpose Driven Life*. Grand Rapids, Mich.: Zondervan.

Scripture Index

SUBJECT INDEX

Share Your Thoughts

With the Author: Your comments will be forwarded to the author when you send them to *zauthor@zondervan.com*.

With Zondervan: Submit your review of this book by writing to *zreview@zondervan.com*.

Free Online Resources at
www.zondervan.com

Zondervan AuthorTracker: Be notified whenever your favorite authors publish new books, go on tour, or post an update about what's happening in their lives.

Daily Bible Verses and Devotions: Enrich your life with daily Bible verses or devotions that help you start every morning focused on God.

Free Email Publications: Sign up for newsletters on fiction, Christian living, church ministry, parenting, and more.

Zondervan Bible Search: Find and compare Bible passages in a variety of translations at www.zondervanbiblesearch.com.

Other Benefits: Register yourself to receive online benefits like coupons and special offers, or to participate in research.